# THE
# NEW GROLIER
# CHILDREN'S
# ENCYCLOPEDIA

## 10

United States of America – Zoology

**GROLIER**
EDUCATIONAL

Published 1999 by Grolier Educational, Danbury, CT 06816
This edition published exclusively for the school and library market

Planned and produced by Kingfisher Publications Plc,
New Penderel House, 283-288 High Holborn, London WC1V 7HZ

2GR/0201/CAC/NEW/JNPI128

Set ISBN 0-7172-9373-4
Volume 10 ISBN 0-7172-9383-1

The new Grolier children's encyclopedia.
p. cm.
Rev.ed. of:The Grolier children's encyclopedia, 1994.
Summary: A ten-volume encyclopedia presenting illustrated articles,
alphabetically arranged, on a wide variety of topics.
ISBN 0-7172-9373-4 (set : alk. paper). —ISBN 0-7172-9374-2
(v. 1: alk. paper). ISBN 0-7172-9375-0 (v. 2: alk. paper).—
ISBN 0-7172-9376-9 (v. 3: alk. paper)
1. Children's encyclopedias and dictionaries. [1. Encyclopedias
and dictionaries.] I. Grolier Educational (Firm) II. Grolier.
children's encyclopedia.
AG5.N34  1998
031—dc21  98-7378
CIP AC

Printed in Hong Kong

# INTRODUCTION

The word *encyclopedia* comes from the Greek for "all-round education," and *The New Grolier Children's Encyclopedia* provides just that, in a way that is both accessible and stimulating.

This all-new encyclopedia covers everything from ancient history to up-to-the-minute developments in technology; from animal and plant life on Earth to plans for the next millennium in outer space. Geography, natural history, religion, the human body—all the topics that children explore at home and at school are included here.

We have rejected the "sound-bite" approach to children's reference in favor of more in-depth coverage, which makes this encyclopedia perfect for project work and homework assignments. At the same time, the text is broken up into manageable paragraphs, suitable for both confident readers and younger browsers. Colorful photographs and superb illustrations and maps not only enhance the text, but also encourage readers to find out more for themselves.

Easy access is the key to this encyclopedia. Major subject areas such as ELECTRICITY have been arranged alphabetically, but the encyclopedia also has a comprehensive index so readers can refer quickly to related topics, such as CIRCUITS and SWITCHES.

The encyclopedia has been written and checked by a team of specialist authors and consultants, and produced by a team of editors and designers with years of experience in children's reference. We are confident that it is a book in which children, and parents, can put their trust.

*The Editors*

*Editorial Director*
Jennifer Justice

**U.S. Consultant**
Bill Shapiro

**U.S. Editor**
Aimee Johnson

*Managing Editor*
Sarah Allen

**Editorial team**
Trevor Anderson, Max Benato, Jane Birch, Harry Boteler, Anne Davies,
Rebecca Fry, Tracey Kelly, Sarah Kovandzich, Elizabeth Longley, Miren
Lopategui, Rupert Matthews, Jayne Miller, Susan Scharpf, Brian Williams

**Creative Director**
Val Pidgeon

*Art Director*
Mike Davis

*Art Editor*
David Noon

**Design team**
Liz Black, Pete Byrne, John Jamieson,
Ruth Levy, Emma Skidmore, Nina Tara

**DTP Operator**
Primrose Burton

**Picture Research**
Veneta Bullen, Davina Bullen,
Sophie Mortimer, Yannick Yago

*Maps*
Hardlines

**Contributors & Consultants**
Sue Aldridge, Sarah Angliss, Max Benato, Martyn Bramwell,
Enid Broderick, Tim Brown, David Burnie, Catherine Halcrow,
Jack Challoner, Michael Chinery, Maria Constantino, Chris Cooper,
Sophie Cooper, Alan Cowsill, Jeff Daniel, David Darling, Dougal Dixon,
John Farndon, Sue Gordon, John Graham, Ian Graham, Catherine Headlam,
Lesley Hill, Caroline Juler, Anne Kay, Robin Kerrod, J.C. Levy, Keith Lye,
Tim Madge, David Marshall, Bob McCabe, Iain Nicolson, Steve Parker,
Jane Parker, John Paton, Malcolm Porter, Sue Reid, Meg Sanders, Philip Steele,
Richard Tames, John Tipler, Ian Westwell, Brian Williams

# UNITED STATES OF AMERICA

**The United States is the world's third largest country in population, and fourth in area. It is rich in natural resources and highly advanced in technology.**

**Area:** 3,618,750 sq. mi.
**Population:** 267,954,767
**Capital:** Washington, D.C. (District of Columbia)
**Language:** English
**Currency:** U.S. dollar

▼ The Statue of Liberty stands at the entrance to New York Harbor. It was a gift from France in 1884 and represents freedom for the people of the United States.

The United States (U.S.) consists of 50 states, 48 contiguous (touching) and 2 apart from the rest. Alaska lies west of Canada and includes Mount McKinley (20,320 ft./6,194m), North America's highest peak. Hawaii is a group of islands in the Pacific Ocean, 2,400 mi. (3,900km) from the U.S. mainland.

### THE 48 STATES

Climate and geography divide the 48 states below Canada into groups from east to west and north to south. Those on the Atlantic coast consist of the New England, Middle Atlantic, and Southern states. The Midwest and Southwest form the center of the country. To the west are the Rocky Mountain states, and west of these are the Pacific Coast states, running south to Mexico.

### VIGOR AND VARIETY

The United States is a country of vast plains and bustling cities, everglades and deserts, spectacular seacoasts, and majestic mountains. Southern plantations grow cotton and tobacco. Midwestern prairies run gold with grain crops. The West Coast has rugged mountains and endless Pacific beaches. Business booms from coast to coast: New

▲ New York is the largest city in the U.S. One of its key symbols is the yellow cab, a common sight on the streets of Manhattan and the other four boroughs.

York and Chicago are major financial centers; Detroit and Cleveland are industrial bases; Atlanta, Dallas, and Houston have become hubs of commerce. Los Angeles and San Francisco dominate the West Coast. The country's historical roots still live in Boston and Philadelphia. Images of Washington, D.C. symbolize the country around the world. New Orleans, Miami, Seattle, St. Louis—all make their unique contribution to the mosaic that is the modern United States. ▶

▲ The Grand Canyon lies in northwestern Arizona. It is one of the most spectacular river gorges in the world, carved from the desert rock by the Colorado River over 6 million years.

1

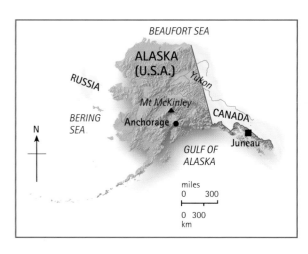

▲ The 800 mi. (1,300km) Trans-Alaska pipeline carries oil from the frozen north of the state to the Gulf of Alaska in the south.

## THE PEOPLE
Since 1940, the population of the United States has more than doubled. Native Americans, who lived in North America for thousands of years before Europeans began arriving, now make up just under one percent of the population. About half of all U.S. citizens are Protestants; nearly a third are Roman Catholics. Jewish people make up two percent of the population; followers of Islam about the same.

## SETTLEMENT AND REVOLUTION
Permanent European settlement of what was to become the U.S. began with a British colony founded in 1607 at Jamestown, Virginia. British colonists spread along America's eastern coast. In the South, they grew tobacco, cotton, and indigo on plantations worked by slaves shipped from Africa. In the North, timber and furs were key products, and fishing was a major industry. French and Spanish explorers and colonists began to settle other territories to the west. Disputes between Britain and its 13 colonies over trade, taxes, and defense led to the Revolutionary War (1775–83), and on July 4, 1776, a group of colonial leaders signed the Declaration of Independence. The war ended in victory for the colonists, led by General George Washington.

## NEW LAWS
In 1787, the Constitution was drawn up and sent to the states for approval. In it, power was divided between the federal government and the individual states. In 1789, a number of amendments that guaranteed specific rights were proposed. Ten were approved by the states and are known as the Bill of Rights. There are now 27 amendments.

▲ The brilliant lights of Las Vegas, Nevada, invite thousands of tourists to enjoy the luxury hotels or try their luck at the world-famous casinos.

▶ About 80 percent of Americans are white or Hispanic. African-Americans form about 12 percent of the population, and Asians, Native Americans, and other groups make up the remaining 8 percent. This classroom reflects the multicultural makeup of the United States.

CANADA

Olympia • Seattle
WASHINGTON • Helena
Salem • Portland
OREGON • Boise
IDAHO
NEVADA
Sacramento • Carson City
San Francisco •
San José •
CALIFORNIA
Las Vegas •
Los Angeles •
San Diego •

Missouri
Rocky Mountains
MONTANA
YELLOWSTONE NATIONAL PARK
WYOMING
Cheyenne
Salt Lake City •
UTAH
Denver
Aspen •
COLORADO
Colorado
GRAND CANYON
ARIZONA
Phoenix •
Santa Fe •
NEW MEXICO
El Paso •
MEXICO

NORTH DAKOTA
Bismarck •
SOUTH DAKOTA
Pierre •
NEBRASKA
Lincoln •
KANSAS
Topeka •
Kansas City
OKLAHOMA
Oklahoma City •
TEXAS
Dallas •
Austin •
San Antonio •
Houston

MINNESOTA
Minneapolis
St. Paul •
IOWA
Des Moines •
ILLINOIS
Springfield •
MISSOURI
Jefferson City
St. Louis •
Little Rock •
ARKANSAS
LOUISIANA
Baton Rouge
New Orleans

Lake Superior
WISCONSIN
Madison •
Milwaukee
Chicago
INDIANA
Indianapolis •
KENTUCKY
Frankfort •
Nashville •
TENNESSEE
Memphis
MISSISSIPPI
Jackson •
ALABAMA
Montgomery •
GEORGIA

MICHIGAN
Lansing Detroit
Lake Michigan
Lake Huron
Lake Ontario
Niagara Falls
Buffalo
Lake Erie
Toledo
OHIO
Columbus •
Charleston •
Springfield
VIRGINIA
Richmond •
Raleigh •
NORTH CAROLINA
Columbia •
SOUTH CAROLINA
Atlanta •
Tallahassee •
Jacksonville •
FLORIDA

MAINE
Augusta •
VERMONT
Montpelier
Concord
NEW YORK
Albany •
Boston
Providence
Hartford
New York
Harrisburg •
Trenton
Pittsburgh •
Cleveland •
Baltimore
Dover
Philadelphia
Annapolis
Washington D.C.

Mississippi
Ohio

ATLANTIC OCEAN

PACIFIC OCEAN

Gulf of Mexico

EVERGLADES
Miami

**KEY TO MAP**
1. NEW HAMPSHIRE
2. MASSACHUSETTS
3. RHODE ISLAND
4. CONNECTICUT
5. PENNSYLVANIA
6. NEW JERSEY
7. DELAWARE
8. MARYLAND
9. WEST VIRGINIA

■ state capital
• major city

N

Kauai
Oahu
Honolulu •
Molokai
Maui
Hawaii
HAWAII (U.S.A.)

miles
0    300
0    300
km

▲ The Midwestern states of North Dakota and Kansas are the country's largest producers of wheat.

## GROWTH OF A NATION
George Washington was the first president, and a new national capital was founded and named in his honor. In 1791, a Bill of Rights was added to the Constitution, guaranteeing the rights of all citizens. In 1802, President Thomas Jefferson bought vast western territories claimed by France, doubling the size of the new nation. In 1804, he sent an expedition to explore the continent from east to west. War against

Mexico (1846–48) led to the conquest of the southwest and Pacific coast. Lured by the discovery of gold in California in 1849 and by the prospect of free land on the prairies, Americans headed west. Washington Irving and other writers helped create a new national identity, and Noah Webster compiled the first dictionary of American English.

## WAR AND PEACE
From 1861 to 1865, America was torn by a civil war which made the South poor, but boosted industry in the North. Peace brought a boom in railroad building. By 1869, railroads joined the East and West coasts. San Francisco, Chicago, and St. Louis grew from frontier posts into great cities. ▶

▼ Surfing and other water sports are popular in the Hawaiian islands, including Oahu, where 80 percent of Hawaii's population lives.

▲ Football, a popular professional and college sport, developed in the 1800s.

▲ The White House had to be rebuilt after it was damaged by fire in the War of 1812.

## INDUSTRY AND IMMIGRATION

Millions of Europeans moved to the U.S., and Native Americans were driven from their traditional lands. America grew rich from its farms and factories. By 1900, the average American was better off than the average European. Half of all Americans still lived on farms, but cities were booming. American inventions, such as the lightbulb, elevator, skyscraper, and airplane, were to change the world.

## A WORLD POWER

In 1867, the United States bought Alaska from Russia. In 1898, it took over the Pacific islands of Hawaii and also went to war with Spain. This led to independence for Cuba and American rule over the Philippines. The U.S. developed a great navy. In 1917, the country joined in World War I to help Britain and France defeat Germany and its allies.

## BOOM, BUST, AND WAR

In the 1920s, the United States was the first country in which millions of people drove cars, listened to the radio, and enjoyed the movies. But the "roaring twenties" ended in a business collapse in 1929, with millions out of work. President Franklin D. Roosevelt used government money from taxes to create new jobs. Following Japan's attack on the naval base at Pearl Harbor (Hawaii) in 1940, Roosevelt led the country during World War II, but died just before the German surrender.

## SUPERPOWER

War boosted industry in the United States and left the country as a superpower, armed with atomic bombs and with a new role as leader of the democratic world. U.S. wealth helped Europe recover from war damage. Today, the United States is the world's most powerful nation, and its culture has spread across the world.

▲ In 1620, a group of English Puritans who called themselves Pilgrims founded a colony at Plymouth, Massachusetts. A recreation of their settlement now stands on the site of the original colony.

◀ In the early 1900s, jazz emerged in New Orleans and developed as a new and distinctly American style of music. Today, the New Orleans jazz festival is world famous.

### SEE ALSO

Bridge, Civil rights, Civil War (American), Cold War, Habitat, Native American, North America, Slavery, World War I, World War II

# UNIVERSE

The universe is made up of stars, planets, and other matter scattered throughout space. It may contain up to 100 billion galaxies with 100 billion stars in each.

Most scientists believe that the universe began with an enormous explosion called the Big Bang, which happened about 15 billion years ago. During this event, all the matter and energy that would ever exist was created in a fraction of a second, in an area smaller than the size of a grape. Ever since the Big Bang, the universe has been expanding outward into space.

▲ NASA put a diagram of humans on a spacecraft, so that it could be found by intelligent life elsewhere in the universe. The dumb-bell represents a hydrogen atom; the symbols below it represent the solar system.

## SEEING INTO THE PAST

A galaxy that is five billion light-years away is seen by astronomers as it was five billion years ago. Therefore, looking at very remote objects gives us a way of seeing the universe when it was much younger than it is today. The most distant objects ever seen are newborn galaxies or galaxies that are still being formed. At even greater distances and earlier times, astronomers can detect only faint radio waves, which come from all parts of space. These are the cooled down remains of the fireball that erupted out of the Big Bang.

## MYSTERIES OF THE UNIVERSE

Scientists ask: will the universe go on expanding forever, or will it eventually begin to shrink and end in a Big Crunch? At present, the answer is unknown, but it seems that the universe may be delicately balanced between the two options. Another question is: does life exist elsewhere in the universe? Again, the answer is not yet known, but the evidence suggests that life may be common throughout space. Space probes sent to other planets search for water, the main ingredient that supports life as we know it. Over 90 percent of the universe consists of dark matter, which cannot be seen. The composition of this remains another great mystery.

## SEE ALSO

Astronomy, Big Bang theory, Galaxy, Planet, Solar system, Star, Time

# VEGETABLE

Vegetables are plants grown to provide food. Most are grown from seeds, bulbs, or tubers, then harvested within a year. A few grow on long-lived plants.

## EDIBLE VEGETABLE PARTS

Eight different parts of vegetable plants are eaten: the bulbs of onion and garlic; the flowers of broccoli and cauliflower; the leaves of lettuce and kale; the roots of carrots and turnips; the seeds and pods of peas and beans; the stems of celery and rhubarb; and the tubers of potatoes and yams. Tomatoes, peppers, eggplants, and squashes such as pumpkins are really fruits, since they contain seeds, but are grown as vegetables.

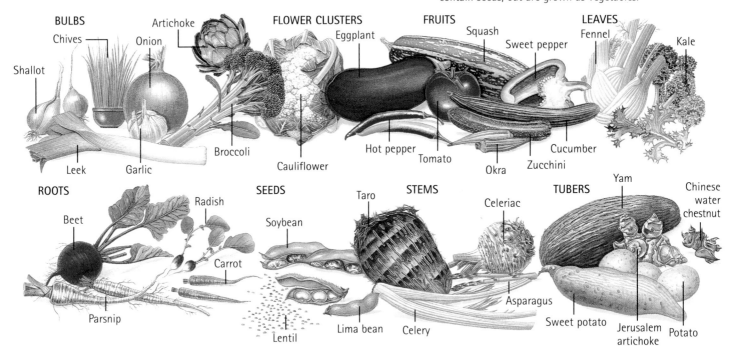

BULBS — Chives — Artichoke — FLOWER CLUSTERS — Eggplant — FRUITS — Squash — Sweet pepper — LEAVES — Fennel — Kale — Shallot — Onion — Broccoli — Hot pepper — Tomato — Okra — Zucchini — Cucumber — Leek — Garlic — Cauliflower

ROOTS — Radish — SEEDS — Taro — STEMS — Celeriac — TUBERS — Yam — Chinese water chestnut — Beet — Soybean — Carrot — Parsnip — Lentil — Lima bean — Celery — Asparagus — Sweet potato — Jerusalem artichoke — Potato

Vegetables are very important to a healthy diet: they are low in fat, and different types provide protein, carbohydrates in the form of starches and sugars, vitamins, minerals, and fiber. Some vegetables, such as potatoes, must be cooked before being eaten; others are best eaten raw, and many vegetables may be eaten either way. Cooking vegetables for too long destroys some of their vitamins.

## SEASONAL VEGETABLES

Vegetables are harvested at different times of the year. Some, like lettuce, are usually eaten fresh, but others, such as peas and beans, can be dried or frozen and cooked later. Root vegetables last for a long time when stored in cool, dry conditions—they can even be left in the soil. Freezing and canning make it possible to eat from a wide selection throughout the year, although fresh vegetables have the highest nutritional value.

## CROPS AND BREEDING

All vegetables contain nutrients. Cultivated crops have more nutrients than their wild ancestors. Many people, particularly in developing countries, have to rely on their own crops for food. If crops fail, they face starvation, so over thousands of years, farmers have selected and bred edible plants that give the best yield for the climate in their area. Through plant-breeding techniques, scientists have developed new varieties of vegetables that are resistant to attack by pests and diseases.

◄ Giant vegetables, such as green beans, are grown for contests, but they are too tough to eat.

## SEE ALSO

Crop, Farming, Nutrition, Plant, Seed and pollination

# VIDEO

Video technology turns moving pictures and sounds into electronic form, stores them on a magnetic tape or disc, then plays them back on a screen.

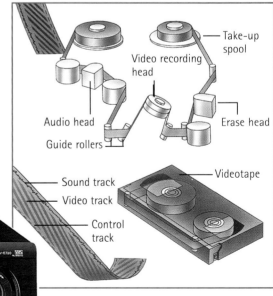

▲ Computer-controlled video-editing setups, using two or more professional VCRs, are used to assemble images and add special effects.

The first videocassette recorder (VCR) was made by Sony in 1969. VCRs record the signal from a TV antenna, satellite dish, cable, or video camera onto magnetic tape. Some video players play videodiscs instead of videotape.

▲ Modern DV (digital video) camcorders store images in digital form. These give high-quality recordings, which can be edited on a multimedia PC.

### GET THE PICTURE

Before video, silent home movies were made using cartridges containing reels of photographic film. These had to be sent off for developing before they could be played back with a projector. Early video systems used a big TV camera connected to a separate, heavy VCR. All this changed in the mid-1980s with the invention of the camcorder (*cam*era-re*corder*)—a portable video camera with a built-in recorder.

### VIDEO CAMERAS

In a camcorder, a lens bends the incoming light to form a sharp image on a flat light sensor called a charge-coupled device (CCD). This turns the image into an electrical signal, which is recorded on tape together with a sound track. The user looks at a viewfinder, which has a small TV or liquid-crystal display (LCD). There are several kinds of tape which can be

▲ Closed-circuit television (CCTV), with small video cameras, is being used increasingly for security surveillance in buildings and public places.

played back through a TV or copied using a VCR. Camcorders are continually getting smaller and lighter, and their quality is improving all the time.

### VIDEOCONFERENCING

The use of video has become increasingly widespread. For instance, video-equipped police cars and traffic cameras help to monitor roads and enforce speed limits. Video telephones never caught on, but videoconferencing over the Internet may become common. This is when tiny video cameras next to computer monitors enable people to see each other as they talk.

### HOW THE VCR WORKS

When recording with a VCR, changes in the incoming signal, which match the changing brightness and colors of the picture, are turned into fluctuating magnetic fields on a recording head. This head spins on a drum and records the magnetic changes on the tape as it moves past. The head crosses the tape diagonally so that the maximum amount of tape is used. During playback, the VCR translates the magnetic changes recorded on the tape back into a picture on a television screen.

Remote control unit

Take-up spool
Video recording head
Audio head
Guide rollers
Erase head
Videotape
Sound track
Video track
Control track

**SEE ALSO**

Computer, Film, Internet, Lens, Photography, Television

# VIKING

The Vikings were a seafaring, warrior people from Norway, Sweden, and Denmark. They invaded northern Europe and explored as far away as North America.

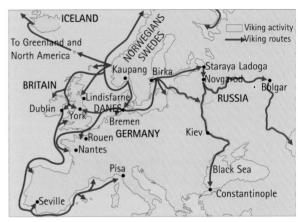

▲ Viking trade and expansion routes in the 800s and 900s ran east through Russia, as far south as Seville and Pisa, and, by A.D. 1000, west to North America.

During the 700s, the population of Scandinavia rose dramatically, but there was not enough land there for farming. At about the same time, the Vikings developed the longship, which gave them the means to reach other lands.

Thor was the Viking god of thunder and war. Thursday is named after him.

### EARLY RAIDS

The first Viking raids were small; one or two longships would raid a few coastal villages and escape with the loot. Around 800, they began to attack in force. They destroyed the monastery on Holy Island (Lindisfarne) and created fear with a series of ferocious attacks from northern France to the coast of Ireland.

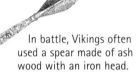

In battle, Vikings often used a spear made of ash wood with an iron head.

### FIERCE RELIGION

Viking gods were fierce and warlike. The Vikings told stories of the gods and heroes in long poems called sagas. They believed the world would end in a war between the gods and giants at Ragnarok ("twilight of the gods"). Odin was their chief god. Men who died bravely in battle were thought to be taken by the Valkyries, 12 handmaidens from Odin's court, to Valhalla, a great hall, to spend eternity feasting and fighting.

A Viking silver amulet in the shape of Thor's hammer and decorated with a face.

### INVASION OF ENGLAND

In 851, Vikings arrived in England with a great army and 350 ships. They invaded Kent, destroying Canterbury. In 866, an even larger Viking army, led by Halfdane and Basecg, invaded Kent. Within five years nearly all of England had been defeated and conquered. The victory of King Alfred the Great (849–99) over Guthrum's Viking army at Edington in 878 saved southern and western England.

### VIKING SETTLEMENTS

Large numbers of Vikings sailed to England and settled in the conquered lands as farmers and traders. York, Lincoln, and Derby became Viking towns. In Ireland, the Vikings founded Dublin and Waterford as trading cities. A large section of northern France—later known as Normandy (from Norsemen)—was captured by Earl Rollo and settled by Vikings. Some Vikings sailed east to travel up the rivers of eastern Europe. At Kiev, they founded a kingdom called the Russ, or Russia.

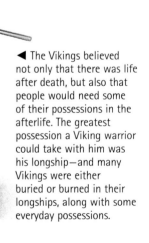

◄ The Vikings believed not only that there was life after death, but also that people would need some of their possessions in the afterlife. The greatest possession a Viking warrior could take with him was his longship—and many Vikings were either buried or burned in their longships, along with some everyday possessions.

▲ Swords were highly valued by the Vikings and were often richly decorated with gold and silver.

## FEARLESS RAIDERS FROM THE SEA

From the late 700s to about 1100, fearless Viking warriors from the Scandinavian countries of Norway, Sweden, and Denmark made several raids on the coasts of Christian countries, inflicting terror on the local inhabitants. They plundered monasteries and churches, killing, burning houses, and driving away the cattle.

## OCEAN VOYAGES

The Vikings were skilled navigators. By studying the stars and the Sun they could travel accurately across vast distances of open sea. In about 825, they reached and settled the Faeroe Islands. Fifty years later, they reached Iceland. There, they founded an assembly—the Althing—to discuss and decide communal matters. The Althing still meets and is the world's oldest governing assembly. In 982, the first Viking settlements on Greenland were established. About the year 1000, a Viking named Leif Ericsson traveled to Newfoundland in

search of timber, which was scarce in Greenland. They continued to visit North America for many years, but the Vikings never settled there.

## VIKING TWILIGHT

By 900, the great Viking raids were over. Wars between Viking settlements and surrounding kingdoms remained common, but most Vikings settled down to a more peaceful existence. The Viking kingdoms in England and Ireland were taken over by the native kingdoms by 970.

## CHRISTIAN CONVERTS

The Vikings and English lived side by side and, for a time, England became part of the Scandinavian Empire, under Canute (1016–35). A last attempt at conquest was made by the Norwegian Viking Harald Hardrada when he invaded England in 1066, but he was defeated and killed. From then on, most of the Vikings adopted Christianity and turned to farming and trading, abandoning raiding and conquest.

▲ A Viking man and woman dressed in everyday clothes.

### SEE ALSO

Myth and legend, Religion, Ship, Warfare

# VOLCANO

**When lava bursts through an opening in the Earth's crust, a volcano forms. The word "volcano" comes from Vulcan, the Roman god of fire and metalworking.**

The Earth's surface is continuously moving through the action of plate tectonics, as sections of the Earth's crust are moved by currents in the molten rock below. There are two types of volcano: basaltic volcanoes found where new plate material is being created, and andesitic volcanoes in areas where plates are being destroyed.

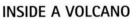

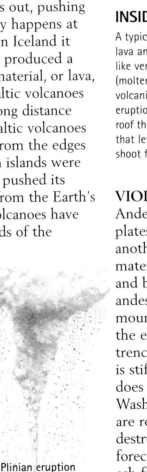

Ash and smoke

Layers of ash and lava

Geyser

Fumarole

Volcanic cone

Caldera

Lava flow

Side vent

Central vent

Magma chamber

▲ Volcanic activity has formed the whole landscape of Iceland. The terrain is littered with jets of boiling water, called geysers.

## BASALTIC VOLCANOES

Where new crust forms along oceanic ridges, the molten material from the Earth's mantle wells up and spreads out, pushing the plates apart. This usually happens at the bottom of the sea, but in Iceland it has risen above the sea and produced a whole island. The molten material, or lava, that erupts from these basaltic volcanoes is very runny and flows a long distance before becoming solid. Basaltic volcanoes are also found a long way from the edges of the plates. The Hawaiian islands were formed as basaltic material pushed its way up through the plate from the Earth's mantle. These "hot-spot" volcanoes have produced many other islands of the Pacific, including the Galapagos Islands and Fiji.

---

**FAMOUS ERUPTIONS**

• In A.D. 79, Vesuvius erupted, destroying the Roman city of Pompeii

• About 90 eruptions have been recorded at Mount Etna, in Sicily, since 1800 B.C.

• Krakatoa, a volcanic island in Indonesia, erupted in A.D. 1883 and killed 36,000 people

• In 1980, the eruption of Mount St. Helens was predicted—the area was evacuated and only a few people died

---

## INSIDE A VOLCANO

A typical volcano has a crater and a cone of solidified lava and ash. Eruptions take place through a chimney-like vent. Far below the surface is a chamber of magma (molten rock), containing bubbling gases that make some volcanic rock frothy. A caldera forms when a violent eruption empties the magma chamber that feeds it. The roof then collapses, leaving a hole. Fumaroles are openings that let out only gas and steam, and geysers sometimes shoot fountains of boiling water high into the air.

## VIOLENT ERUPTIONS

Andesitic volcanoes are found where plates are being drawn beneath one another and destroyed. Molten plate material rises through the overriding plate and bursts through at the surface. These andesitic volcanoes occur in the great mountain chains, and in island arcs around the edges of oceans, close to deep ocean trenches. The lava of an andesitic volcano is stiff and sticky, and when it erupts, it does so explosively. Mount St. Helens, in Washington, and the island of Montserrat are recent examples of such violent and destructive eruptions. Because of accurate forecasting, few were killed, but the hot ash from Mount St. Helens destroyed trees up to 19 mi. (30km) away.

Vulcanian eruption

Plinian eruption

Hawaiian eruption

Volcano cones created by Hawaiian eruptions slope gently, because the lava flow is quite runny

A vulcanian eruption, after Vulcano, in Italy, throws almost solid magma during an explosion

Plinian eruptions, such as the one that destroyed Pompeii in A.D. 79, explode with great clouds of ash and pumice

---

**SEE ALSO**

Earth, Earthquake, Mountain and valley, Ocean and sea, Rock

---

# WARFARE

**Warfare is armed conflict between the military forces of two nations or states, or between organized groups within a state.**

Much of recorded history is a recounting of war and conflict. This is often because one group seeks to impose its will on another for some form of gain, such as territory, food, or natural resources.

## TURNING TO ARMS

Wars start for different reasons. The Crusades and the Thirty Years' War, in the 1600s, started for religious reasons. In 1701, the Ashanti fought for freedom from another African people and created a great trading nation. The Indian Wars of the late 1800s saw Native Americans defending their way of life against those who wanted their land. Involvement in Korea and Vietnam stemmed from opposition to communism in the Cold War.

## OUTBREAK OF WAR

Countries going to war want to appear to be in the right. This encourages citizens to support the war, and deters other countries from helping the enemy. Often a relatively minor incident will trigger a war.

▲ Samurai warriors used their discipline and skill with weapons to control Japan from 1200 to 1871.

In 1914, the Hapsburg Empire declared war on Serbia after a Serb killed the Austrian archduke. But the Hapsburgs really wanted to stop Serbia encouraging unrest within the empire.

## INTELLIGENCE

Once at war, commanders need to know about the strengths and plans of the enemy. The lack of such knowledge left France vulnerable to the German attack of 1940. Information may be gathered by watching the enemy from satellites and aircraft, by capturing or decoding messages, or by using spies. Information would then be given to commanders to help make battlefield decisions. ▶

Ancient Egyptians used stone for maceheads, knives, and arrowheads and spearheads.

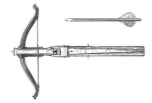

Medieval crossbows shot bolts accurately, but were slow to load and use.

## OARS AND RAMS

The Battle of Salamis in 480 B.C. was fought between the oared galleys of Greece and the Persian Empire. The Greeks defeated the larger Persian fleet because their *triremes* (ships with three banks of oars) were faster and easier to handle than the Persian ships.

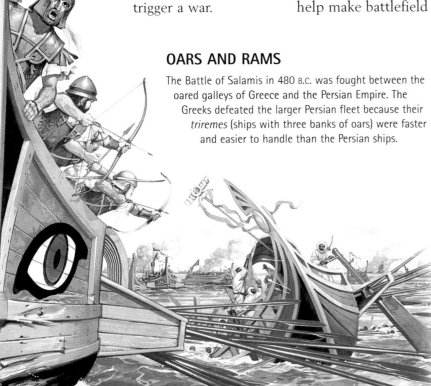

▲ Hand weapons of the Middle Ages included:
1 Daggers for stabbing; 2 Maces to crack metal armor; 3 War hammers, used as maces; 4 Spiked staffs; 5 Pikes with handles up to 6.5 ft. (2m) long to keep horsemen at a distance.

## TOTAL WAR

In a total war, an entire country is organized for fighting. In the Zulu Empire, during the 1800s, every young man had to serve in the army and boys, older men, and women provided supplies. Both world wars of the 1900s were total wars. Men were conscripted into the armed forces, and many industries switched to producing weapons. It was considered fair to bomb cities in which factories were located, even though this might mean killing civilians.

▲ In Europe in the 1400s, armor covered the body with carefully shaped metal plates, each curved and ribbed to deflect blows.

▲ Helmets fringed with chain mail gave protection while allowing movement.

## THE FATE OF PRISONERS

Prisoners are taken in all wars, but their treatment has differed. The Romans sold prisoners as slaves. The Aztecs sacrificed prisoners to their gods. During the 1800s, in wars with the British, the Afghans tortured all prisoners to death—the British often shot their men if they could not rescue them. World War II prisoner of war camps in Japan were notorious for

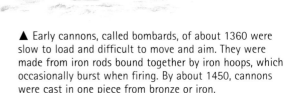

▲ Early cannons, called bombards, of about 1360 were slow to load and difficult to move and aim. They were made from iron rods bound together by iron hoops, which occasionally burst when firing. By about 1450, cannons were cast in one piece from bronze or iron.

bad conditions. The Geneva Convention of 1864, and its later revisions in 1906, 1929, 1949, and 1977, lays down strict rules about prisoners of war. They cannot be tortured. They must be given the same food and shelter as their captors, and they cannot be forced to do work to help the war effort. Prisoners are usually released at the end of a war.

## LIMITED BLOODSHED

War by its nature is violent. Soldiers may kill civilians, steal goods, and burn houses, so attempts have been made to reduce the violence. During the 1100s, the idea of chivalry encouraged knights to avoid hurting women or children and to take prisoners rather than killing captives. In 1631, the German city of Magdeburg was captured by an army of Croats and Walloons. The soldiers looted the city and slaughtered thousands. European monarchs were appalled and developed

### KEY DATES

c.5000 B.C. Cities in Mesopotamia form first armies

c.90 B.C. Marius reforms the Roman armies into professional and full-time forces

c.800 Feudal armies made up of semiprofessional knights form in Europe

c.1350 Gunpowder is invented

1916 Tanks are used for the first time

1945 Nuclear weapons are used for the first time

1991 The first major use of cruise missiles in the Gulf War by the United States

## THE BATTLE OF WATERLOO

The Battle of Waterloo was fought in 1815 between the French, led by Napoleon Bonaparte, and a joint British, Dutch, and German army. The muskets and cannons of the time had only a limited range. The colorful uniforms helped soldiers tell friend from foe in the smoke of the battlefield.

the idea of limited war, which meant that civilians were to be unharmed and armies could surrender peacefully.

## OBEYING THE RULES

Many wars have been fought according to a set of rules. In Ancient Greece, most cities depended on olive oil for food, so olive trees were usually not destroyed when an enemy city was captured. The people of each city knew that they might be defeated at some time, and wanted to have enough food to survive. During the Middle Ages, prisoners were given a chance to buy their freedom immediately by paying a ransom.

## WAR CRIMES

Before 1945, any enemy soldier or leader who broke the rules of war was hanged or put in prison. At the end of World War II, the Allies set up special courts to try

▲ In 1906, HMS *Dreadnought* was a new type of battleship, armed with 12-in. guns and able to steam at over 20 knots (30 mph). Battleships remained the most powerful ships afloat until aircraft carriers in the 1940s.

people as war criminals for breaking the Geneva Convention and for the mass murder of Jews and others in the Holocaust. In the 1990s, new war crimes courts were set up to try people who had killed civilians during the Bosnian civil war.

## GUERRILLAS

Some wars are fought by irregular troops called guerrillas. Such wars are usually fought when the enemy is too strong to be faced in battle. Using any weapons at hand and operating in small groups, ▶

▲ The British Mark IV tank of World War I was designed to crush barbed wire and cross trenches while protecting its crew from machine-gun fire.

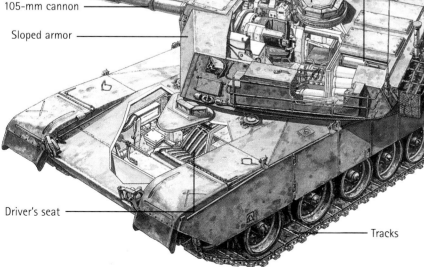

Commander's hatch and periscopes — Ammunition store

Engine

Machine gun

105-mm cannon

Sloped armor

Driver's seat

Tracks

A handgun of 1400.

A 1500s' wheel lock.

A 1600s' flintlock.

The Colt revolver of 1851.

A matchlock musket.

A breechloading rifle of the 1800s.

The German Mauser pistol of 1896.

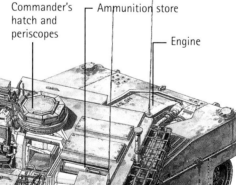

The Gatling gun of 1862 was an early machine gun.

A German 50-ton siege cannon of 1867.

## THE MAIN BATTLE TANK

The Abrams M1 is the main battle tank (MBT) of the United States. MBTs are any army's most important weapon. They have guns up to 120mm caliber that are able to destroy strongholds and enemy tanks; armor protects the crew from all but the heaviest guns; mobility allows them to move through enemy territory to reach targets.

Modern warships have guns, missiles, and complex electronics.

The Mustang was the fastest American fighter of World War II.

The German V1 could fly 150 mi. (240km) with a 2,000 lb. (900kg) warhead.

The American Honest John missile can reach a range of 12.4 mi. (20km).

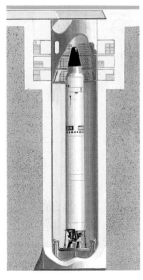

Modern Intercontinental Ballistic Missiles (ICBMs) carry nuclear warheads.

## U.S. NAVY TOMCAT

The Grumman F14-A Tomcat is a twin-engined, two-seater fighter designed to fly from aircraft carriers to protect the U.S. fleet from enemy bombers.

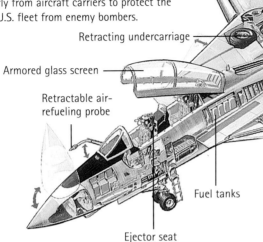

Wing pivot mounting

Retracting undercarriage

Armored glass screen

Retractable air-refueling probe

Fuel tanks

Ejector seat

guerrillas cut enemy supply lines and ambush patrols. The aim is to wear down the enemy forces, so that they give in.

## PSYCHOLOGICAL WEAPONS

Many commanders try to persuade the enemy to surrender or to retreat by tricking them. In the 1740s, Frederick the Great of Prussia had a special regiment of men over 7 ft. (2.2m) tall. Because he only used his "giants" when he thought he would win, enemies seeing them advancing would think they were beaten. In World War II, British aircraft dropped leaflets on Germany urging troops to surrender. They failed because the leaflets contained obvious lies.

## RADIO TRICKS

During World War II, a British radio station aimed at German troops claimed to be broadcast by a German army officer. Because the "officer" used army slang, many Germans believed the stories of German defeats. Tokyo Rose, a Japanese radio show, mixed stories of American defeats with popular music during World War II.

## PEACEFUL SOLUTIONS

At the end of every war is a period of peace. This is often agreed between the two sides in a document called a treaty. Treaties set out conditions, such as the handing over of territory and the return of prisoners, which are signed by all parties. The Treaty of Amiens ended a war between Britain and France in 1802, but it left so many issues unresolved that the two were at war again just one year later. Other treaties have been more successful. The Treaty of Vienna in 1815 was signed by every nation in Europe and meant that peace lasted for decades. After World War II, the United Nations was set up to solve international disputes with the aim of preventing war from breaking out.

▶ Soldiers of the U.S. 82nd Airborne Division wear gas masks during the Gulf War of 1991. Chemical and biological weapons can cause massive casualties.

**SEE ALSO**

Castle, Celt, Civil war, Crusades, Greece (Ancient), Mongol Empire, Napoleonic Wars, Rocket, Roman Empire, United Nations, World War I, World War II

# WATER

Water is the most common substance on Earth. It is the main ingredient in all living organisms—without water, life on the planet could not exist.

## WATER FACTS

- A person drinks over 15,800 gal. (60,000 l) of water in a lifetime

- Human beings will die if they lose more than 20 percent of the body's normal water content

- It takes about 21 pt. (10 l) of water to flush a toilet; 37 gal. (140 l) to fill a bathtub; nearly 11 gal. (40 l) to wash the dishes; and up to 32 gal. (120 l) for a washing machine

- The wettest place on Earth is Cherrapunji in India, with an average annual rainfall of 426 in. (10,820mm)

▲ Three fourths of the world's fresh water is frozen in glaciers and polar ice caps.

## THE WATER CYCLE

Water is constantly being recycled. When the Sun heats the Earth's surface, water evaporates into the atmosphere. Over 80 percent of this comes from seas, but some comes from plants giving off water vapor (transpiration). As water in the atmosphere cools, it condenses to form clouds. Some of this water falls again as rain.

Water vapor condenses and forms clouds

Rain and snow

Transpiration from plants

Water vapor in atmosphere

River flows back to oceans

Evaporation from seas and lakes

Water vapor cools and forms rain

Groundwater runs off

Water vapor        0.05 percent
Moisture in soil   0.2 percent
Rivers and lakes   0.35 percent
Saltwater lakes
and inland seas    0.4 percent

22% Groundwater

Ice caps and glaciers 77%

Fresh water 3%

Seawater 97%

▲ Of the 3 percent of the world's water that is not in the seas, 77 percent is locked in ice and glaciers.

Water exists naturally in three different forms: solid (frozen as ice), liquid (water), and gas (water vapor in the air). It can dissolve more substances than any other liquid. The force of natural water power has shaped the world's mountains, valleys, coastlines, and plains.

## UNIVERSAL SUBSTANCE

Water covers 70 percent of the Earth's surface—over 5.6 billion cu. mi. (1.4 billion cu km)—but only a tiny fraction is of use to humans. Almost 97 percent of all water is seawater, with up to about 77 lb. (35kg) of dissolved salts in every ton—eight times too salty to drink or to use for crops. Only about three percent of all water is fresh—and three fourths of that is in polar ice caps and mountain glaciers. Every living thing depends on the small amount of fresh water (under one percent of the total) that falls as rain and fills rivers and lakes.

## WATER FOR LIVING

Life began in the sea 3.5 billion years ago, and water is still essential for all life-forms. The human body consists of about two-thirds water. People need 5 pt. (2.5 l) of water a day to stay alive, but in the West, we use about 66 gal. (250 l) each per day for bathing, toilets, and washing machines. We also use vast amounts of water in industry and agriculture. It takes 105 gal. (400 l) of water to grow enough wheat for one loaf of bread, and 270 tons of water to produce a ton of steel.

## SHAPING THE LAND

Water is the most important force in shaping the land. Rivers and glaciers carve valleys, wear down mountain ranges, and carry gravel, sand, silt, and clay onto lowland plains and eventually out into the sea. Even spectacular desert scenery is carved mainly by water from flash floods.

## SEE ALSO

Lake, Mountain and valley, Ocean and sea, River, Waterpower, Weather

# WATERPOWER

Waterpower uses the movement of water to turn machinery or to generate electricity. It is a renewable, nonpolluting source of energy.

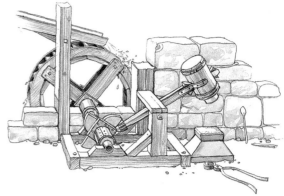

▲ In the Middle Ages, waterwheels were used to power hammers for ironworking. They saved time and labor.

Waterwheels have been used to grind grain into flour since the time of Ancient Greece. In Britain in the 1800s, they provided the power for big textile mills during the Industrial Revolution. Electric generators that could convert the turning motion of a waterwheel into electricity led to the rapid development of hydroelectric power in the early 1900s.

### HYDROELECTRIC POWER

Water is first stored in a reservoir, often made by damming a river and flooding its valley. The water flows down pipes through turbines, propellerlike blades that are spun around by the flow of the water. In turn, these spin the electric generators. Pumped storage plants can push the water back up into the reservoir using off-peak electricity, then generate electricity again when demand is high, like charging up a giant battery. About 20 percent of the world's electricity comes from hydroelectric power, but it is available mainly in mountainous areas, far away from large cities, where most of the power is needed.

▲ A huge wave crashing against the shore shows the awesome force of natural waterpower. The sea can be harnessed to generate electricity in tidal power plants and wave-power generators.

### TIDAL POWER

Dams built across river estuaries trap the rise and fall of ocean tides. The trapped water turns turbines as it flows through holes in the dam. These use the "head" of water made by the rise and fall of ocean tides to spin turbines. The largest tidal power plant, on the Rance River in Brittany, France, has been generating 240 megawatts of electricity since 1966.

### WAVE POWER

The up-and-down movement of sea waves can be used to make electricity, but this is more difficult than using flowing water to turn a turbine. Wave-powered electric generators began operating in the 1980s. One plant, built on the Clyde River in Scotland, generates only two megawatts of electricity, but larger plants are planned.

### TURBOGENERATOR

Water flows past turbogenerators inside the dam wall of a hydroelectric power plant. A turbogenerator converts the energy of flowing water into electrical energy. The shaft is turned by the pressure of water against its curved blades, and this moves the generator rotor, which generates (produces) an electric current.

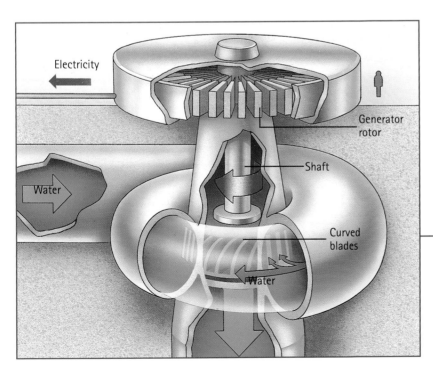

Electricity

Generator rotor

Shaft

Water

Curved blades

Water

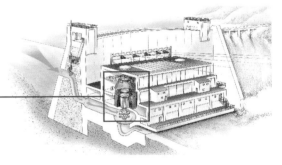

### SEE ALSO

Dam, Electricity, Energy, Engine, Water

# WAVELENGTH

**Wavelength is the distance between two identical points on a wave. This is usually measured from one peak of the wave to the next.**

Most of us have seen waves on the sea. Before they reach the coast, these waves make the seawater ripple. The highest points of these ripples are called peaks, the lowest points are called troughs. The distance between one peak and the next is called the wavelength of the waves.

### SOUND WAVES
All forms of moving energy, including sound, light, and heat, travel in waves. All of them have a wavelength just like waves on the sea. When sound waves travel through air, for example, they create tiny changes in the air pressure. The peaks of a sound wave are where the air pressure is greatest. Our ears pick up the changes in air pressure and send signals to the brain.

### DIFFERENT WAVELENGTHS
Just like frequency (the rate at which a wave moves up and down), wavelength affects a wave's properties because wavelength and frequency are closely related. For instance, low-frequency sound waves have a longer wavelength than high-frequency ones. Similarly, red light waves have a longer wavelength than blue ones. Light is one of a range of energy waves, including radio waves, microwaves, infrared rays, ultraviolet rays, X rays, and

gamma rays, all of which travel at 483,000 mi./sec. (300,000km/sec). Together, these form the electromagnetic spectrum.

▲ Police often use radar to catch speeding motorists. Radar waves from a gun bounce off a moving vehicle. The frequency at which they return gives its speed.

### WAVELENGTH AND FREQUENCY
If you divide the speed of a wave (measured in meters per second) by its frequency (measured in Hertz), you can work out its wavelength (in meters). For example, a sound wave that travels at 344m/sec and has a frequency of 688 Hz has a wavelength of 0.5m (because 344 ÷ 688 = 0.5).

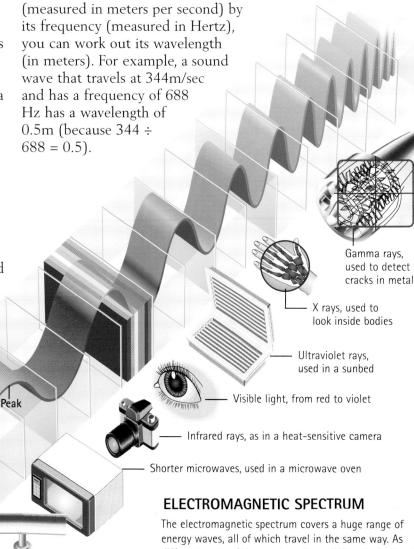

Wavelength

Peak

Trough

Gamma rays, used to detect cracks in metal

X rays, used to look inside bodies

Ultraviolet rays, used in a sunbed

Visible light, from red to violet

Infrared rays, as in a heat-sensitive camera

Shorter microwaves, used in a microwave oven

Longer microwaves, used in radar

Ultrahigh Frequency (UHF) radio waves for TV transmissions

Radio waves used in radio broadcasts

### ELECTROMAGNETIC SPECTRUM
The electromagnetic spectrum covers a huge range of energy waves, all of which travel in the same way. As different parts of the spectrum have different wavelengths, they have different properties. A light wave, for example, is one that we can see. An X ray is a part of the spectrum that can pass through some solid objects, such as skin.

### SEE ALSO
Energy, Light, Musical instrument, Radar and sonar, Radio, Sound, X ray

# WEATHER

Atmospheric conditions, such as rain, wind, and sunshine, make up the weather at a particular place and time. Weather may change slowly or rapidly.

An anemometer is used to measure the speed of the wind. Its sensitive shells move in the wind's path.

A barograph records changes in air pressure on a rotating drum, using an inked pen to draw a graph.

The psychrometer uses a dry bulb and a wet bulb to measure the humidity in the air.

Thermometers measure air temperature. They are used either inside or outside buildings.

The weather depends on the way air masses move around the globe. The climate of a place is the average of these weather conditions over a long period of time. Though weather may change within hours, climates change over years.

## CAUSES OF WEATHER

The way that air masses are driven depends on factors such as distance from the equator and the presence of mountains or seas. When an air mass moves from the sea over high ground, it cools, and the water it contains falls as rain. If an air mass moves from the center of a continent, it contains no water and brings dry weather. If a mass of air rests over tropical waters for a long time, it becomes extremely moist and warm, leading to severe storms.

## REGULAR CYCLES

The weather follows regular cycles. In many areas, the summer means warmer weather than the winter because more solar (sun) energy is received during long, hot days. In Southeast Asia, the monsoon period is dominated by warm, wet winds from the Indian Ocean, causing heavy rains. Every ten years or so, a phenomenon called El Niño occurs: the temperature of the southeast Pacific Ocean rises slightly, which alters the movements of air masses. This can lead to drought, severe rainstorms, and economic disaster.

Stratus cloud

Temperature

Drizzle

Rain

Sleet

Dry snow

Wet snow

When water freezes, its molecules bind together into a flat, six-sided crystal, with four long sides and two short ones. The crystal grows as other water molecules attach themselves to its sides. Each snowflake is unique.

▲ When rain clears quickly after a shower, a colorful rainbow may stretch across the sky. Sunlight shines on water droplets, and light is bent, or refracted, until it is split into spectrum colors.

▲ Inside a storm cloud, raindrops may be carried up by air currents and frozen in the clouds. Layers of ice build up as water vapor freezes onto these icy crystals. The growing hailstones fall to warmer levels, then rise again until they are heavy enough to fall from the clouds.

## RAIN AND SNOW

Two main types of rain occur. In the tropics, rain forms when tiny droplets come into contact in a cloud, join together, and fall. Rain outside the tropics is caused by melting snowflakes. If the base of a stratus cloud is low enough, rain falls as drizzle. Dry snow falls when the ground temperature is cold, but if snow falls into air that is above freezing, sleet (a mixture of rain and snow) occurs.

18

**1** The Sun heats one area of ground, such as bare soil, more than others. On warm days, bubbles of hot air form over these areas, and rise up through the cooler air around them.

**2** Warm air rises into low-pressure air, then expands and cools. The air cools so much that water vapor condenses into droplets, and a small cumulus cloud is formed.

**3** As it is fed by a series of air bubbles, the cloud grows, and the wind detaches it. Fair-weather cumulus clouds look like cotton balls. They do not carry enough water to cause rain.

▲ Radiosondes are balloons that carry instruments to measure temperature, air pressure, and humidity in the upper atmosphere.

## HIGH AND LOW PRESSURE

In most parts of the world, weather is determined by areas of low air pressure (cyclones) or areas of high pressure (anticyclones). Some last for months; the Bermuda High is an anticyclone that appears in the North Atlantic during the summer. Others last only a few days or weeks. In tropical areas, belts of low pressure can be massive and move slowly westward. As they suck in warm air, heavy rain and storms are created.

## FRONTS

When a mass of cold air meets a mass of warm air, a front develops. If cold air cuts sharply under warm air, a cold front forms. The warm air rises rapidly, cools, and produces heavy rains. If warm air rises slowly, it produces a warm front marked by long periods of gentle rain and drizzle.

## DESTRUCTIVE WEATHER

Although most thunderstorms are harmless, a large storm can produce strong winds, heavy rain, lightning, and hail. In 1986, a storm in Gopalganj, India, created a downpour of hailstones weighing 2.2 lb (1kg) each, killing 100 people in a few seconds. Lightning kills around 200 people a year and starts over 20,000 fires. Tornadoes form when thunderstorms create strong updrafts. The spinning air can reach 310 mph (500kph) and wreak destruction along a path 0.6 mi. (1km) wide and 62 mi. (100km) long.

## FORECASTING

Traditionally, people have forecast weather either by watching the sky or noticing the behavior of animals, which is affected by basic weather changes. Modern weather forecasting is based on the global movement of areas of low and high pressure and fronts, which is tracked using satellite photographs.

◀ ▲ As water droplets collide in a large cloud, water becomes electrically charged. Positive charges collect at the cloud's top, and negative charges at the bottom. As a negative charge meets a positive charge on the ground, forked lightning flashes; sheet lightning flashes between clouds. Thunder is the sound of hot air expanding.

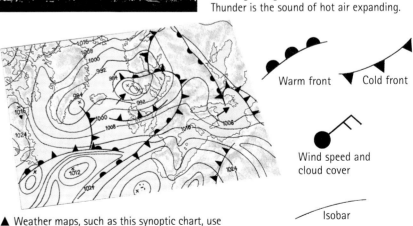

▲ Weather maps, such as this synoptic chart, use standard symbols. Isobars are lines that connect places where air pressure is the same. Winds flow parallel to isobars; the closer together they are, the stronger the wind. Air pressure (in millibars) is shown at centers of low and high pressure. Wind speed, and warm and cold front symbols, are also shown.

Warm front    Cold front

Wind speed and cloud cover

Isobar

### SEE ALSO

Climate, Ecology, Electricity, Light, Satellite, Season, Water

19

# WEIGHTS AND MEASURES

**Weights and measures are the standard units that we use to work out how much we have of things. Each form of measurement needs its own kind of "ruler."**

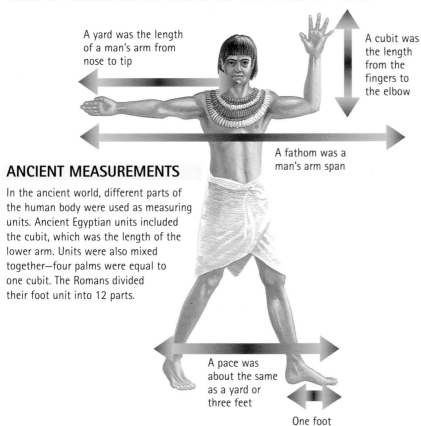

A yard was the length of a man's arm from nose to tip

A cubit was the length from the fingers to the elbow

A fathom was a man's arm span

A pace was about the same as a yard or three feet

One foot

## ANCIENT MEASUREMENTS

In the ancient world, different parts of the human body were used as measuring units. Ancient Egyptian units included the cubit, which was the length of the lower arm. Units were also mixed together—four palms were equal to one cubit. The Romans divided their foot unit into 12 parts.

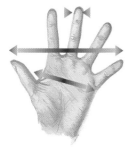

▲ Units based on the hand included the digit, which was the width of a finger. This later became the inch. A span was the length from thumb to little finger, and there was also the palm unit.

Ever since people started making things, trading goods, or carrying out experiments, they have needed to measure amounts. Ancient civilizations based their measurements on parts of the body. These were standard (the same) only within each civilization. An Egyptian cubit, for example, was different from a Greek or Roman cubit. This caused many problems, especially when people needed to trade with one another. That's why, over time, standard measurement systems have come into use.

## TRADITIONAL MEASUREMENTS

Until about 30 years ago, most people used the imperial system of measurement. This measured length in inches, feet, yards, and miles; and weight in ounces, pounds, and tons. The use of the foot as a unit of measurement dates back to Anglo-Saxon times. The inch (3 grains of barley, lengthwise) dates to the 1300s, when it was established as one twelfth of a foot. The mile has its origins in measuring thousands of paces. Ounces and pounds are units of the *avoirdupois* ("goods sold by weight") system, in use since at least the 1400s. The imperial system isn't always easy to use, however, and people who took complex measurements realized they needed a simpler system. In the 1790s, the metric system was created in France.

## METRIC SYSTEM

Many countries use the metric system, or SI (Système International). The basic units are the meter (length) and the kilogram (weight). There are many other units with their own special names such as the joule, the newton, and the volt. However, scientists can relate most of them to the basic set: one newton (1N), for example, the unit of force, can also be written as one kilogram meter per second per second ($1kg\ m/sec^2$).

## SETTING STANDARDS

A laboratory near Paris holds examples of the SI units—the Standard Meter is the length of a certain number of wavelengths of a specially made laser beam. The Standard Kilogram is the weight of a special ingot of platinum-iridium metal, stored at a controlled temperature.

▲ Scales have been used to weigh objects for sale for thousands of years. Here, they are used to weigh dried flower and plant remedies for sale at an herbalist dispensary.

## WEIGHT

**Metric**

| | | |
|---|---|---|
| 1,000 milligrams (mg) | = | 1 gram (g) |
| 1,000 grams | = | 1 kilogram (kg) |
| 100kg | = | 1 quintal (q) |
| 1,000kg | = | 1 metric ton or tonne (t) |

**Standard**

| | | |
|---|---|---|
| 16 ounces (oz.) | = | 1 pound (lb.) |
| 112 lb. | = | 1 hundredweight (cwt.) |
| 20 cwt. | = | 1 (long) ton (= 2,240lb.) |
| 2,000 lb. | = | 1 short ton |

**Conversions**

| | | |
|---|---|---|
| 1 gram | = | 0.035oz. |
| 1kg | = | 2.205 lb. |
| 1 metric ton or tonne (t) | = | 2,200 lb. |
| 1t | = | 0.984 (long) tons |
| 1 oz. | = | 28.35g |
| 1 lb. | = | 454g |
| 1 (long) ton | = | 1.02t |

## AREA

**Metric**

| | | |
|---|---|---|
| 100 square mm (mm$^2$) | = | 1 square cm (cm$^2$) |
| 10,000cm$^2$ | = | 1 square metre (m$^2$) |
| 100m$^2$ | = | 1 are (a) |
| 100a | = | 1 hectare (ha) |
| 100ha | = | 1 square kilometre (km$^2$) |

**Standard**

| | | |
|---|---|---|
| 144 square inches (in.$^2$) | = | 1 square foot (ft.$^2$) |
| 9 ft.$^2$ | = | 1 square yard (yd.$^2$) |
| 4,840 yd.$^2$ | = | 1 acre |
| 640 acres | = | 1 square mile (mi.$^2$) |

**Conversions**

| | | |
|---|---|---|
| 1cm$^2$ | = | 0.155 in.$^2$ |
| 1m$^2$ | = | 10.76 ft.$^2$ |
| 1 hectare | = | 2.47 acres |
| 1km$^2$ | = | 0.386 square miles |
| 1 in.$^2$ | = | 6.45cm$^2$ |
| 1 ft.$^2$ | = | 0.093m$^2$ |
| 1 acre | = | 0.405 hectares |
| 1 sq. mi. | = | 2.59km$^2$ |

## LENGTH

**Metric**

| | | |
|---|---|---|
| 10 millimeters (mm) | = | 1 centimeter (cm) |
| 100cm | = | 1 meter (m) |
| 1,000m | = | 1 kilometer (km) |

**Standard**

| | | |
|---|---|---|
| 12 inches (in.) | = | 1 foot (ft.) |
| 3 ft. | = | 1 yard (yd.) |
| 1,760 yd. | = | 1 mile (mi.) |

**Conversions**

| | | |
|---|---|---|
| 1mm | = | 0.0394 in. |
| 1cm | = | 0.394 in. |
| 1m | = | 1.094 yd. |
| 1km | = | 0.621 mi. |
| 1 in. | = | 2.54cm |
| 1 ft. | = | 30.48cm |
| 1 yd. | = | 0.914m |
| 1 mi. | = | 1.609km |

## VOLUME

**Metric**

| | | |
|---|---|---|
| 1,000mm$^3$ | = | 1 cubic centimeter (cm$^3$) |
| 1,000cm$^3$ | = | 1 cubic decimeter (dm$^3$) |
| 1,000dm$^3$ | = | 1 cubic meter (m$^3$) |

**Standard**

| | | |
|---|---|---|
| 1,728 cubic inches (in.$^3$) | = | 1 cubic foot (ft.$^3$) |
| 27 ft.$^3$ | = | 1 cubic yard (yd.$^3$) |

**Conversions**

| | |
|---|---|
| 1cm$^3$ = 0.06 1 in.$^3$ | 1m$^3$ = 35.3 ft.$^3$ |
| 1 in.$^3$ = 16.4cm$^3$ | 1 ft.$^3$ = 0.028m$^3$ |

## CAPACITY

**Metric**

| | | |
|---|---|---|
| 1,000 milliliters (ml) | = | 1 liter (l) |
| 100 liters | = | 1 hectoliter (hl) |

**Standard**

| | | |
|---|---|---|
| 4 gills | = | 1 pint (= 16 fluid ounces) |
| 2 pints | = | 1 quart |
| 4 quarts | = | 1 gallon |

**Conversions**

| | |
|---|---|
| 1 liter = 0.908 quart | 1 pint = 0.473 liters |
| 1 deciliter = 0.21 pint | |

The Egyptians used delicate balancing scales to weigh gold and precious stones. Later, the Babylonians (who lived in what is now Iraq) made standard weights from metal to use at markets.

The builders of the pyramids in Egypt had to measure length so that they knew how many stones they needed, as well as how to drive shafts accurately through the huge structures.

The measuring cup is used to measure liquids in fluid ounces (imperial units) and milliliters (metric units). Wine bottles usually hold 700 or 750 milliliters (ml) of wine when they are full.

### SEE ALSO

Babylon, Clock, Gravity, Time

# WHALE AND DOLPHIN

Whales, dolphins, and porpoises are collectively known as cetaceans, which means "large sea animal." They are divided into two groups: toothed and baleen whales.

A white-sided dolphin eats fish and has 92–128 teeth. It is found in large schools of up to 1,000 dolphins.

A rough-toothed dolphin is a small (up to 8 ft./ 2.5m), tropical species known to follow ships.

Common porpoises are one of the smallest cetaceans (up to 6.5 ft./ 2m). There are six species.

There are about 37 species of dolphin; 23 species of large-toothed whale; ten species of baleen whale; and six types of porpoise. They may look like fish, but whales and dolphins are warm-blooded, air-breathing mammals.

## FROM EARTH TO SEA

Whales first appeared on the Earth over 50 million years ago. Their ancestors once lived on land, but then moved into the water and gradually lost their back legs; their front legs became flippers. The flippers are used for steering and balance, but the power comes from the big tail with its horizontal fins or flukes. The tail is waved up and down to drive the whale forward. (Fish have vertical tail fins, waved from side to side.)

▶ Black right whales belong to the right whale family of three species. They reach 60 ft. (18m) in length and are rare.

◀ Fin whales belong to the rorqual and humpback family that have grooved throats. They grow to 66 ft. (20m).

▶ Bowhead whales grow up to 60 ft. (18m) and their baleen plates can be 9 ft. (3m) long. They belong to the right whale family.

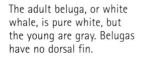

The adult beluga, or white whale, is pure white, but the young are gray. Belugas have no dorsal fin.

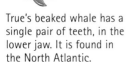

True's beaked whale has a single pair of teeth, in the lower jaw. It is found in the North Atlantic.

A male bottle-nosed dolphin grows up to 13 ft. (4m). It eats squid, cuttlefish, and herring.

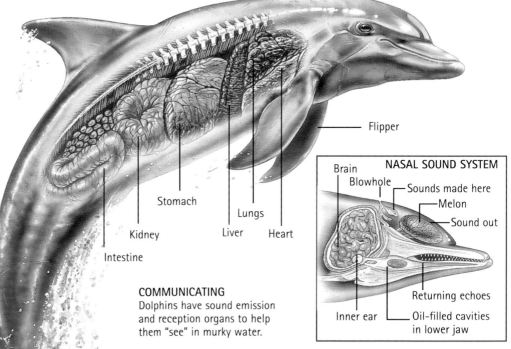

Flipper

Stomach

Kidney

Intestine

Lungs

Liver

Heart

### COMMUNICATING
Dolphins have sound emission and reception organs to help them "see" in murky water.

**NASAL SOUND SYSTEM**

Brain
Blowhole
Sounds made here
Melon
Sound out
Returning echoes
Inner ear
Oil-filled cavities in lower jaw

## SEEING WITH SOUND

Dolphins communicate, find food, and navigate using a kind of radar sound system under water. They make high-frequency clicking noises by blowing air through their nasal passages. Then the melon (a waxy cavity in the dolphin's head) focuses the sound into a beam. Sound vibrations travel through the water and bounce off objects. A dolphin receives the sound echoes through an area in its jaw where the bones are thinner. The echoes then travel to the inner ear.

## STRAIN OR BITE

There are two types of whale: baleen whales and toothed whales. Baleen whales are filter feeders that strain tiny creatures from the water through fringed curtains of a horny material called baleen or whalebone.

◀ Blue whale.

▲ The number and size of teeth varies with species. Dolphins (above) have conical, interlocking teeth, porpoises have spade-shaped teeth, and most beaked whales only have two visible pairs.

## THERE SHE BLOWS

Whales come to the surface to breathe. As they breathe out, warm moist air rushes out through nostrils on the top of the head—the blowhole. This "blow" may reach 33 ft. (10m) into the air. They then take a few breaths through the blowhole and dive down for several minutes. Toothed whales have just one blowhole, baleen whales have two.

## FRIENDLY GIANT

The blue whale is the largest animal that has ever lived on Earth. It can reach a length of 100 ft. (30m) and a weight of 150 tons—as heavy as 20 full-grown elephants. Like most of the other large whales, the blue whale has no teeth. It is a baleen whale that feeds on tiny plankton and krill living near the surface of the sea. Other whales and dolphins have many teeth and feed on fish, squid, seals, and penguins.

## SMILING DOLPHINS

Dolphins are small whales with a pointed snout and appear to have a permanent smile. They are playful and intelligent animals. They live in groups called schools and communicate with clicks and whistles. They use sound location to navigate and find fish to eat. An injured dolphin will usually be helped by other members of the school. There are even reports of dolphins helping drowning people. Like all whales, dolphins never come ashore. They mate and give birth to their young in the sea. A mother dolphin feeds her baby on her milk for a year and they often stay together for several years.

▲ Narwhals grow up to 18 ft. (5.5m) with no dorsal fin and two teeth. In males, one tooth develops into a spiral tusk up to 9 ft. (2.7m) long.

◀ Sperm whales are a family of three species. They are the largest toothed whales (growing to 66 ft./20m) and the deepest divers. They eat mostly squid.

◀ Orcas, or killer whales, are dolphins with a tall (6 ft./2m) sharklike fin. They have long, sharp teeth and eat young whales, seals, squid, or fish.

**SEE ALSO**

Animal, Conservation, Mammal, Migration

# WIND

Wind is the movement of air over the Earth's surface. It can range from a gentle summer breeze to the destructive power of a hurricane or tornado.

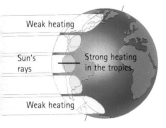

▲ The sun is strongest in the tropics, where it is almost overhead. Closer to the poles, the sun's rays are more spread out and therefore weaker.

North Pole (high pressure)

South Pole (high pressure)

▲ Wind is the flow of air from high- (H) to low-pressure areas (L). This creates six main bands of air across the globe.

Wind is the movement of air from an area of high pressure to an area of low pressure. A wind is named after the direction from which it is blowing. So a north wind is one blowing from the north.

## BLOWING HOT AND COLD

Big global wind systems such as the trade winds and easterlies are caused by the heating effect of the sun. Near the equator, the sun is almost overhead, and so the land, sea, and air receive the maximum amount of heat. Warm air tends to rise (just as a hot-air balloon rises), and because it is rising, it does not press down so much on the Earth's surface. This creates a low-pressure area. Colder, heavier air sinks down toward the Earth's surface in cooler regions, farther from the equator, and this creates high-pressure areas. The cooler, heavier air flows over the Earth's surface from high-pressure areas to low-pressure areas, creating winds.

▲ Hurricanes form in the late summer and fall over warm areas in the Atlantic, Pacific, and Indian oceans. They then move westward, along the coasts.

## LOCAL WINDS

Local winds arise from a combination of weather patterns and the shape of the land. Land heats up and cools down quicker than water, and this produces the gentle breezes you often feel at the coast. During the day, the land heats up, the air above it warms up and rises, and moist air flows in from the sea to replace it, creating a cool sea breeze. At night, the land cools quickly, the air above it descends and spreads out, and this produces a light offshore breeze. Other local winds form around mountains, especially where there are glaciers. At night, cold, heavy air pours down the hillsides and valleys, and out over the surrounding lowlands.

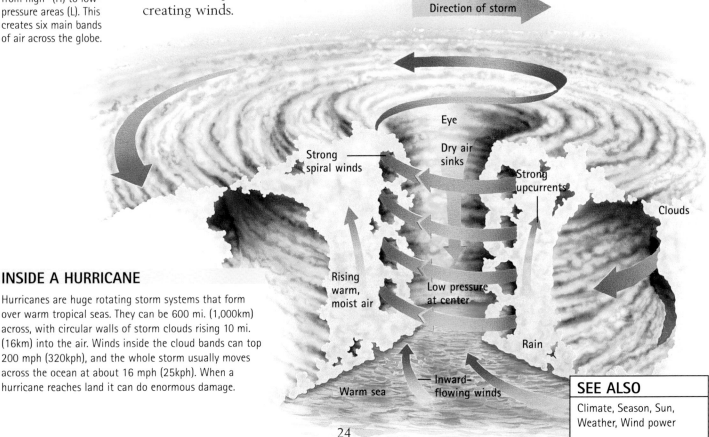

Direction of storm

Eye

Dry air sinks

Strong spiral winds

Strong upcurrents

Clouds

Rising warm, moist air

Low pressure at center

Rain

Inward-flowing winds

Warm sea

## INSIDE A HURRICANE

Hurricanes are huge rotating storm systems that form over warm tropical seas. They can be 600 mi. (1,000km) across, with circular walls of storm clouds rising 10 mi. (16km) into the air. Winds inside the cloud bands can top 200 mph (320kph), and the whole storm usually moves across the ocean at about 16 mph (25kph). When a hurricane reaches land it can do enormous damage.

**SEE ALSO**
Climate, Season, Sun, Weather, Wind power

# WIND POWER

Wind power uses the power of the wind to turn machinery or generate electricity. It is a renewable, nonpolluting source of energy.

Fantail

▲ The addition of a fantail, invented in 1745, automatically turned the top of the mill so that the sails caught the wind.

Windmills have been used to grind corn or pump water from the ground for hundreds of years. Simple windmills may have been used in Ancient Persia (now Iran) in the A.D. 600s. Modern windmills, called wind turbines, use the turning motion of the blades to spin a turbine, which generates electricity.

### SPINNING SAILS
In a windmill, four to eight wind sails, each 10–30 ft. (3–9m) long, catch the wind. As they spin, a shaft turns. Gears transfer the power to turn a heavy grinding stone at the bottom of the building. Spring sails made of wooden shutters, invented in 1772, could be adjusted to turn steadily in varying winds.

### WIND TURBINES
Windmills were largely replaced in the 1900s by engine power. But wind turbines are a growing energy source. Pioneered in Denmark in the 1890s, they use airfoils like airplane propellers to

▲ Although often only 1,600 ft. (500m) across, tornadoes unleash a devastating force. They form over land, like dark funnels of cloud, and can contain winds of over 250 mph (400kph)—strong enough to demolish buildings and throw cars around like toys.

turn a turbine and make electricity. Used to supply electricity in remote areas, wind farms may have hundreds of wind turbines, with blades 50–100 ft. (15–30m) in diameter. The largest wind farms can generate up to 1,120 megawatts, as much electricity as produced by a nuclear power plant. Although nonpolluting, wind farms use great areas of land.

### WIND FARMS
Wind turbines need to be made so that they turn, even in gentle wind, and also cope with gales. They also need to be built where there is plenty of wind, such as along the coast or on flat plains. These places are usually a long way from where the electricity is needed, and much energy is lost sending it along power lines.

### FAST FACTS
• The sailboat is one of the most common users of wind power

• The largest wind farms are in California, and can generate over 1,000 megawatts of power on a windy day

• By 2050, 10 percent of the world's electricity may be generated using wind power

### SEE ALSO
Boat, Electricity, Wind

# WOLF AND OTHER WILD DOGS

**Wolves, coyotes, jackals, and foxes are all kinds of wild dog. They are strong, quick, alert carnivores, many of which hunt in packs.**

A skillful hunter, the red fox lives in Asia, Europe, and North America.

In winter, the long fur of the Arctic fox turns from brown or gray to white.

Known for its eerie howl, the coyote is found in Canada, the U.S., and Mexico.

Wolves belong to the group known as *Canidae*, or the dog family. This group also includes the gray, red, and maned wolf, coyote, and dingo, African and Asian (dhole) wild dogs, raccoon and bush dogs, 4 kinds of jackal, about 20 kinds of fox—as well as the hundreds of breeds and varieties of domestic dog. These were probably tamed and bred from wolf ancestors at least 10,000 years ago.

## FEATURES OF THE HUNTER

All members of the dog family are meat-eaters, or carnivores. They live by hunting or scavenging. But they eat almost anything if they are hungry, even fruits and berries. They have acute senses, including sharp eyesight and hearing, and an excellent sense of smell. Their long, strong legs, which they use for fast running and relentless pursuit, have clawed toes for good grip and scratching. Their long, sharp teeth bite and tear flesh.

## WHERE WOLVES LIVE

The gray, or timber, wolf, usually just known as the wolf, is widespread across North America, parts of Europe, the Middle East, and northern Asia. It prefers forests but can live in mountains, grasslands, and even deserts. The red wolf is extremely rare, limited to a small area of

◀ When gathering to begin a hunt, wolves greet each other with loud howls. This warns wolves from other packs to stay out of their territory.

▲ In each pack, some wolves are more dominant than others. Here, a dominant wolf stands with its tail and ears held up, while a subordinate wolf approaches it in a crouched position, tail between legs and ears flattened.

southeast North America. The maned wolf, which is really more like a long-legged fox, dwells in grassy scrubland in central South America.

## WILD DOGS AROUND THE WORLD

The coyote, with its mournful howl, is a wolflike wild dog that has extended its territory from the southwestern United States and Mexico. In Australia, the dingo is probably descended from the part-tamed dogs of Aboriginal people, brought to the continent more than 7,000 years ago. Jackals live across Africa, the Middle East, and southern Asia. Different kinds of bushy-tailed fox dwell in almost every habitat, from the Arctic fox of the snowy far north, to the Cape fox of southern Africa's deserts, and the well-known, widespread, and adaptable red fox, which scavenges trash in towns and cities.

### KEY FACTS

• Various members of the dog family can breed with each other. For example, a domestic dog and a coyote produce coydog puppies. This interbreeding makes it difficult to know exactly how many true species are in the dog family

• The main difference between wolves and dogs that look like them is that wolves carry their tail hanging down while dogs carry it curled up

• The crab-eating fox of South America really does eat crabs, and tortoises, too, but it prefers easier meat, such as mice, birds, lizards, insects, and eggs

## HUNTING IN PACKS

Many wild dogs, especially wolves and African and Asian wild dogs, hunt with others of their kind. The group is called a pack. It can catch much larger prey than one dog hunting alone. A pack of wolves can bring down a full-grown moose over 6.5 ft. (2m) high. Each pack has dominant males, or leaders, who get the best food and mate with females at breeding time.

## A VARIETY OF PREY

Other wild dogs, especially foxes, live and hunt alone, or with a mate. Jackals have a reputation as scavengers. In fact, they usually hunt live prey—from frogs, lizards, and mice to small gazelles and young zebras. Smaller wild dogs usually eat smaller meals. Most foxes have a diet of mice, voles, fish, frogs, birds, eggs, and insects. The smallest kind, the fennec fox, with huge ears, survives in the Sahara and Middle Eastern deserts by consuming small beetles, spiders, locusts, and worms.

▲ The dingo, which can be bred with the domestic dog, howls, but rarely barks. Dingoes come together to run down and kill large prey, such as kangaroos.

## A DOG'S LIFE

Wolves have long been feared in legend and have therefore been persecuted. In fact, wolves attack people only when threatened or if they are extremely hungry. Many other wild dogs are also hunted, and some are endangered. People shoot, poison, or trap them in case they raid farm animals. Also some kinds, especially foxes, are still killed for their handsome fur pelts.

The jackal is up to 30 in. (75cm) in length. It has a strong body smell.

The raccoon dog lives throughout eastern Asia and is mainly nocturnal.

The African wild dog lives in large parts of Africa, and hunts its prey in packs.

## PACK HUNTERS

Wolves hunt in packs, feeding on almost any animal that they can catch. In order to kill prey such as reindeer and elk, which are faster and stronger than they are, wolves must be quick and skillful. Wolves hunt by day and by night, roaming through territory until they find prey. They stalk it by moving toward it against the wind to prevent it from picking up their scent. Once close enough, the wolves break into a run and the chase begins. If they succeed in catching their victim, they weaken it through injury, then grab it by the throat.

**SEE ALSO**

Animal, Desert, Dog, Mammal

# WOMEN'S RIGHTS

Women's rights are those civil rights that have traditionally been denied to women in many societies. Women have had to struggle to gain these rights.

**MARY WOLLSTONECRAFT** (1759–97), Irish–English writer of one of the first feminist books, *Vindication of the Rights of Women* (1792). A later pamphlet, *Thoughts on the Education of Daughters* (1797) criticized girls' schooling.

**ELIZABETH CADY STANTON** (1815–1902), organized the first women's rights assembly in the U.S. in 1848. She fought for fair property and divorce laws for married women, coeducation, and the right to vote (suffrage).

**EMMELINE PANKHURST** (1858–1928), a women's rights leader in the U.K., founded the Women's Social and Political Union (1902) campaigning for the right to vote. She and her daughter, Christabel, were imprisoned many times.

In different societies the status of men and women has varied greatly. Today it is generally thought that men and women should have equal rights, and some countries have laws to make forms of discrimination (unfair treatment) illegal.

## ANCIENT RIGHTS

The role of women within society has varied greatly. In Ancient Greece, women had few rights. They were expected to stay at home and to take no part in social life. Some Greek teachers believed it was wrong to teach women to read in case they learned too much and disagreed with the men. In Egypt, however, women played a full part in society. They could take jobs, own property, and divorce their husbands. Some became rulers, but usually after the death of a husband.

## DIVISION OF LABOR

In traditional farming communities, the work of a family was divided. Men mainly carried out heavy physical work. Women took on household tasks and childcare. Other jobs in society were also divided.

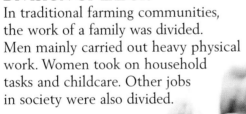

▶ The U.S. Army 24th Infantry in Saudi Arabia. The Gulf War, in 1990–91, was the first conflict that saw women soldiers of the U.S. Army fighting alongside men.

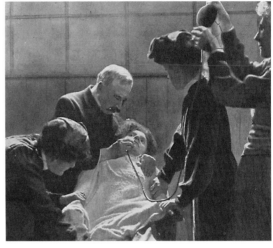

▲ Imprisoned women's rights campaigners in the U.K. went on hunger strikes and were brutally force-fed.

Traditionally, men fought in the army, while women often cared for the sick.

## CHANGING RIGHTS

Industrial revolution in the 1800s brought changes. The work in many new industries did not need strength, but skill. Women were able to do many factory jobs just as well as men. A family could be supported by a woman instead of a man. By the late 1800s, most industrialized nations had

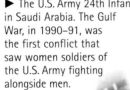

civil rights for women. Women were allowed to keep their own property when they married, instead of giving control to their husbands. They could enter into contracts and sign legal papers, teach, and become nurses and doctors, although education for girls was still less formal than for males and ended at an earlier age.

## THE VOTE

For a long time only those who owned property could vote. During the 1800s, this was challenged. The right to vote (suffrage) was extended to poor men, but not to women. In 1869, Elizabeth Cady Stanton and Susan B. Anthony founded the National Woman Suffrage Association; in the same year Lucy Stone set up the rival National American Woman Suffrage Association. Activists were called suffragists. In the U.K., Emmeline Pankhurst organized the Women's Social and Political Union; U.K. activists were called suffragettes.

## SLOW PROGRESS

Women in New Zealand were the first to get the vote, in 1893—but Maori women had to wait until 1967. By the 1920s, most democracies had given women the vote, although Swiss women won it only in the 1970s. Women in some Muslim countries are still not equal to men and cannot vote or stand for election.

## SHIFTING HORIZONS

During the 1960s, a movement called Women's Liberation sought to make women equal to men in social and economic terms. Gradually women's choices have widened. Today there are women doctors, lawyers, and judges. The number of women running companies is slowly rising. It is not unusual to see women as bus drivers, firefighters, or construction workers. Women have taken frontline roles in some Western armies. Even so, balancing a career and motherhood is still a dilemma for many women.

▲ During the two world wars, many Western women took jobs making weapons in factories. It was their war efforts that led to greater recognition of women's value.

▲ Israel's Golda Meir was deputy foreign minister in 1948, and later foreign minister. She became the Israeli prime minister in 1969.

◀ In 1996, the Taliban (fundamentalist Muslims) took over the government of Afghanistan. They banned girls from schools, women from working, except in women's projects, made women cover themselves, and segregated the sexes.

## SEE ALSO

Civil rights, Democracy, Education, Industrial Revolution, Israel, Textile, World War II

# WORLD WAR I

World War I was a terrible war fought between 1914 and 1918 in which millions of people died. It began in Europe, but spread to many parts of the globe.

Kaiser Wilhelm II (1859–1941) of Germany led an aggressive foreign policy against other nations.

Lloyd George (1863–1945), British prime minister from 1916, reorganized the war effort for victory.

Russia's Tsar Nicholas II (1868–1918) backed Serbia against Austria, bringing Russia into the war.

People living at the time called World War I "the Great War" because no other war had been so widespread nor so destructive. Millions of soldiers were killed and the world economy changed for ever.

## OUTBREAK OF WAR
In 1914, Europe was divided into two major alliances. The Hapsburg Empire was allied to Germany to block Russian moves in the Balkans, while France sided with Russia against the growing might of Germany. On June 28, 1914, the Hapsburg archduke Franz Ferdinand was shot dead by a Serb terrorist, prompting the Hapsburgs to declare war on Serbia. Serbia, in turn, asked for help from the Russians, who then declared war on the Hapsburgs. This brought Germany and France into the war. Britain joined the war when Germany invaded Belgium.

## EARLY BATTLES
In the east, Russian armies were smashed by the Germans at Tannenberg, while Hapsburg armies were defeated by the Russians in several encounters during the month of September. In the west, the Germans intended to capture Paris and defeat France, but were stopped on the Marne River on September 8, 1914, while the British army blocked outflanking moves to the North. By October, the armies had settled into trenches for the winter.

## NEW WEAPONS
Barbed wire barriers, machine guns, and artillery made defense so strong that attacks were almost useless. Troops experimented with poison gas to help attackers, but it rarely had much effect. Tanks, first used by the British in 1916,

▲ World War I began after Serb terrorist Gavrilo Princip killed the Hapsburg archduke Franz Ferdinand. Princip was sentenced to 20 years in prison, but got sick and died in 1918.

could defeat barbed wire or machine guns, but they often broke down. Aircraft were more successful, and were used to spy on enemy troops, target artillery shells, and drop bombs. The German pilot Manfred von Richthofen, nicknamed the "Red Baron," successfully shot 80 enemy aircraft down in flames.

## WORLD WAR
In Africa, British and French troops attacked German colonies. In 1915, Australian and New Zealand troops attacked Turkey at Gallipoli, but were badly defeated and sustained heavy losses. At sea, German ships and submarines sank Allied ships, and in 1917 began attacking any ships heading for Allied ports. The United States first protested about these attacks on its ships, and then joined the Allies, declaring war on Germany.

▲ Trench warfare led to small battlefronts. Only on the Eastern Front were sweeping movements made.

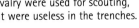

◄ Russian Cossacks and other cavalry were used for scouting, but were useless in the trenches.

Aircraft were a new weapon, used for scouting and fighting.

## KEY DATES

**August 1914** War breaks out between the Allies (France, Britain, Russia, Belgium, Serbia, and Montenegro) and the Central Powers (Germany and the Hapsburg Empire)

**November 1914** Turkey joins the Central Powers

**May 1915** Italy joins the Allies

**October 1915** Bulgaria joins the Central Powers

**August 1916** Romania joins the Allies

**April 1917** The United States joins the Allies

**December 1917** Russia makes peace with Germany

**November 1918** Fighting ceases

**1919** Peace Treaties signed at Versailles in France

The small Serb army was driven out of Serbia into Greece in December 1915.

## FINAL MOVES

In 1917, the Communists took over Russia and made peace. The German troops, freed from Russia, launched a massive attack in March 1918 in France. American troops helped to stop the attack. But Bulgaria, Turkey, and the Hapsburgs were close to collapse and Germany asked for peace. A ceasefire was finally agreed on November 11, 1918.

## TRENCH WARFARE

The war in the West was fought from trenches guarded by barbed wire and machine guns. Conditions were appalling, with knee-deep mud, constant shelling, sniping, and raids. The battles of the Somme and Verdun in France in 1916 cost over two million casualties, although neither side managed to advance more than a few hundred yards.

## THE WAR ENDS

The cost of World War I was immense. Germany lost 1.9 million men, Russia 1.7 million, France 1.5 million, and Britain and the Hapsburgs 1 million each, as well as vast amounts of money. The Hapsburg Empire was split into Austria, Hungary, Czechoslovakia, and Yugoslavia. Poland, Estonia, Latvia, and Lithuania became independent. European countries lost economic power as others built up their industries. The world was changed for ever.

Britain had the smallest army in 1914, but it was made up of professionals.

Machine gun post in the French trenches

German troops

In 1914, the German army was the largest and best trained in the world.

**SEE ALSO**

Communism, Empire, Warfare, World War II

# WORLD WAR II

**World War II was fought between 1939 and 1945. It involved more countries, cost more lives, and caused more destruction than any other war.**

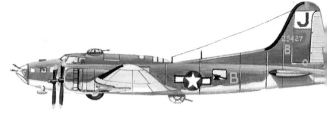

The American B17 Flying Fortress

Erwin Rommel (1891–1944) was a daring leader of German armored units.

Adolf Hitler in Germany, Benito Mussolini in Italy, and General Tojo Hideki in Japan wanted to extend the power and territories of their countries. They formed a pact, called the Axis, to gain what they wanted.

The Japanese Mitsubishi Ki-67, codenamed "Peggy"

## BLITZKRIEG

In September 1939, Germany invaded Poland to regain land it had lost in World War I. Britain and France supported Poland. The Germans used a tactic called *blitzkrieg*—lightning war. Bomber aircraft began the attack, then tanks, or panzers, plunged deep behind enemy lines, followed by infantry and artillery. Poland was defeated in just five weeks. In April 1940, Hitler invaded Denmark, Belgium, Holland, Norway, and France. By July, only Britain had not surrendered. In the Battle of Britain, the determined Royal Air Force beat off German air attacks.

Yamamoto Isoroku (1884–1943) planned Japan's attack on Pearl Harbor.

The German Dornier Do217

The British Lancaster

▲ Small bombers, such as the Dornier and Mitsubishi, were used to destroy battlefield targets, such as tanks and artillery. The Lancaster, Flying Fortress, and other heavy bombers pounded cities and factories.

Bernard Montgomery (1887–1976) led the British in North Africa and Europe.

## INTO RUSSIA

Hitler wanted to expand Germany and create *lebensraum* ("living space") for the German nation. In June 1941, 3.5 million German, Italian, Romanian, and Hungarian troops stormed into Russia, capturing vast territories. In December, a reinforced Red Army finally stopped the invaders just outside Moscow.

## PEARL HARBOR

Japan wanted to capture large areas of Southeast Asia to secure industrial raw materials. The Japanese hoped that a quick defeat would persuade the United States to allow Japanese expansion, so they launched a surprise attack on Pearl Harbor. The U.S. did not give way, but declared war. The same day, Japan invaded Southeast Asia. By May 1942, Japan had conquered Burma, Malaya, the Philippines, and the East Indies.

Georgy Zhukov (1896–1974) commanded the Soviet Red Army.

### THE TIDE TURNS

After three years of war, the Allies had built up their armed forces. In North Africa, German and Italian troops were defeated at El Alamein in October 1942, and in December 1942, the German 6th Army was

Dwight D. Eisenhower (1890–1969) led the D-Day invasion of 1944.

◀ On December 7, 1941, 360 Japanese aircraft attacked Pearl Harbor, Hawaii, the base of the U.S. Pacific Fleet. The attack opened the way for Japanese conquests and brought the U.S. into the war.

► Germany, Japan, and their allies made large conquests in 1939–42. But the greater resources of the Allies were brought into action after 1942.

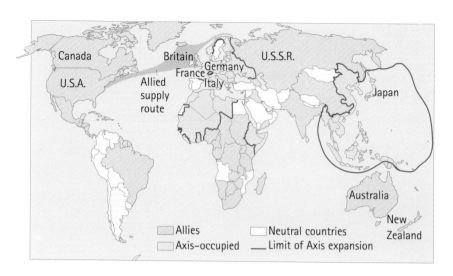

wiped out at Stalingrad. The Japanese were halted in February 1943. The Allies then organized strike forces to retake Burma, and to use island-hopping tactics in the Pacific.

## GERMANY COLLAPSES

In June 1944, Germany was caught between the Normandy landings and the Russian advance. On April 30, 1945, Hitler killed himself; two days later Germany surrendered. The Allies found that the Nazis had murdered millions, six million of them Jews, in the worst case of mass human extinction in history. It has come to be called the Holocaust. Jewish people refer to it as the Shoah, meaning "chaos" or "annihilation."

## THE ATOMIC BOMB

With the war over in Europe, President Truman wanted to bring U.S. troops home from the Pacific—Japanese forces were determined to fight on. To end the war and cut casualties, the U.S. decided to use the atomic bomb. It obliterated the cities of Hiroshima and Nagasaki; 200,000 people died. Japan surrendered on September 2, 1945.

## PEACE AND COLD WAR

The war had cost the lives of some 15 million troops and 35 million civilians. After the war, the world divided into two powerful blocs: the communist countries, led by the Soviet Union and China, and the democratic world, led by the United States. The Cold War had begun.

▲ The Allied leaders, Winston Churchill (left), Franklin D. Roosevelt (center), and Joseph Stalin, met at Yalta in 1945 to decide the postwar arrangements for Europe.

## D-DAY

At dawn on June 6, 1944, the largest invasion fleet in history landed Allied forces on the coast of Normandy. In all, 1,200 warships and 4,100 landing craft put 132,500 soldiers ashore, while 10,000 aircraft attacked German positions inland. The success of the D-Day invasion allowed American, British, and French troops to drive the Germans out of France.

## SEE ALSO

Cold War, Fascism, Great Depression, Warfare, World War I

# WORM

Worms are legless invertebrates (animals with no backbone). There are four major groups: ribbon worms, flatworms, roundworms, and segmented worms.

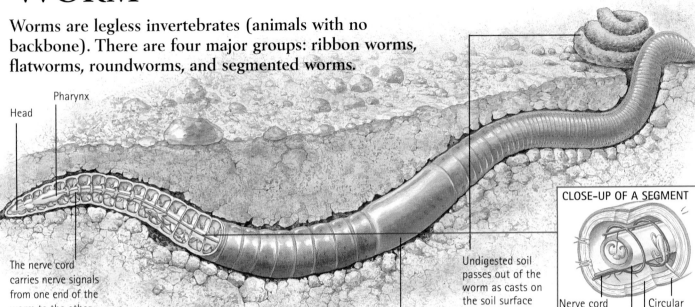

Head

Pharynx

The nerve cord carries nerve signals from one end of the worm to the other

Clitellum—produces cases for worm eggs

Undigested soil passes out of the worm as casts on the soil surface

**CLOSE-UP OF A SEGMENT**

Nerve cord

Intestine

Circular muscle

Longitudinal muscle

A lugworm (segmented) has feathery gills.

A horse leech (segmented) can grow to 1 ft. (30cm).

Flatworms can cause serious illnesses in humans.

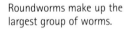
Roundworms make up the largest group of worms.

Ribbon worms live in the sea and can be 6.5 ft. (2m).

A ragworm (segmented) has strong jaws to eat prey.

There are thousands of kinds of worm. The simplest, such as flatworms, are found mostly in the sea or are parasites that live inside animals and humans. Ribbon worms are like long flatworms— the bootlace worm grows to 85 ft. (25m).

## EARTHWORMS

The earthworms that tunnel in gardens belong to a group called annelids, or segmented worms. Their bodies are made of many ringlike sections. There are hundreds of species of earthworm and all feed by swallowing soil and digesting any decaying matter in it. They also pull dead leaves into their tunnels and eat them. Earthworms are important for farmers and gardeners because their tunnels drain and bring air into the soil and allow plant roots to grow. There are no separate male and female worms: each one has both male and female parts. After mating, which usually takes place above ground at night, each worm lays its own eggs.

## BLOOD-SUCKING LEECHES

Leeches are related to earthworms, but instead of having bristles for moving they have a large sucker at each end. Most of them live in water or damp soil and feed on other animals. Some of the bigger ones are bloodsuckers and may attack people.

## SLITHERING SEGMENTS

Each segment of an earthworm's body has several little bristles on the underside and these enable the worms to move through their tunnels. The bristles of one group of segments dig into the walls like anchors while powerful muscles push or pull the others forward. There are no lungs; respiration takes place through the body surface.

## PARASITIC WORMS

Many flatworms and roundworms (also called nematodes) live inside other animals as parasites. Hooks or suckers on their head cling to the lining of the host's intestines and the worms soak up digested food. Tapeworms, which can reach 98 ft. (30m), produce many eggs, which pass out with the host's droppings. Some eggs find their way into new host animals.

▲ Peacock worms live in the sea. They catch food with bristles and live in a tube made from secretions.

**SEE ALSO**
Animal, Blood, Earth, Sight, Zoology

# X RAY

X rays are a form of energy that can pass straight through many solid materials. We use X rays to look inside bodies and machines and to kill some cancers.

▲ X-ray radiation was discovered by the German physicist Wilhelm Roentgen (1845–1923), who was awarded the first Nobel Prize for Physics in 1901.

▼ High doses of X rays can damage body cells. The harmful effects of X rays are often used to help cure cancers. Powerful beams of X rays are directed at cells in a tumor, killing them off.

If you break a bone, you will probably go to the hospital for an X ray. An X-ray image lets the doctor see where your bone is fractured or damaged. A special machine directs a narrow beam of X rays at the part of your body that needs examining. Unlike light waves, these X rays can pass right through the soft parts of your body, the skin and muscles.

## X-RAY IMAGE

When X rays come through your body, they hit a photographic plate, where they form an image. Because your bones and teeth are heavy and dense, they block the path of the X rays. This is why they leave blank areas on the X-ray image. Trained people can look at these blank areas and work out the exact shape of your skeleton.

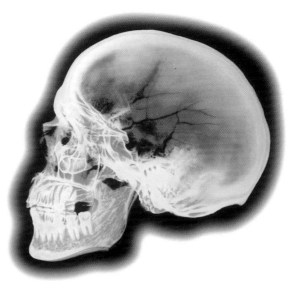

▲ This X-ray image of a human skull found at a Roman burial site reveals a missing top molar tooth.

## SOFT TISSUE

Sometimes, doctors use X rays to look at softer, lighter parts of your body, such as the liver or bladder. To do this, they inject you with a special chemical called barium sulfate. This makes these tissues block the path of X rays. The body gets rid of this chemical naturally after a few hours.

## MACHINES AND CRYSTALS

X rays are not only used to look inside people. They are also used to examine the insides of certain machines. Aircraft makers, for example, take X-ray images of various machine parts to make sure they have no inner cracks. Chemists take X-ray images of crystals. They use these to study how the X rays bounce off a crystal's inner structure. This can help them work out how the atoms in the crystal are arranged.

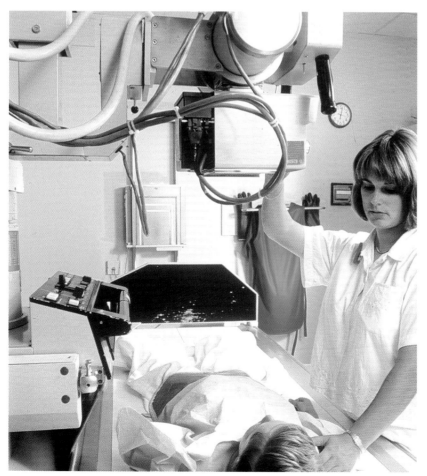

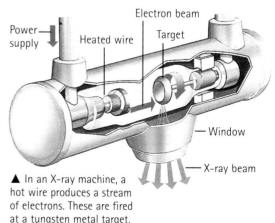

Power supply — Heated wire — Electron beam — Target — Window — X-ray beam

▲ In an X-ray machine, a hot wire produces a stream of electrons. These are fired at a tungsten metal target, giving out X rays. Some pass through the patient's body, making an image on film or a fluorescent screen.

### SEE ALSO

Astronomy, Atom and molecule, Light, Medicine, Wavelength

# ZOOLOGY

Zoology is the scientific study of all animals—their body structure, how they live, feed, breed, move, and behave—in nature or captivity.

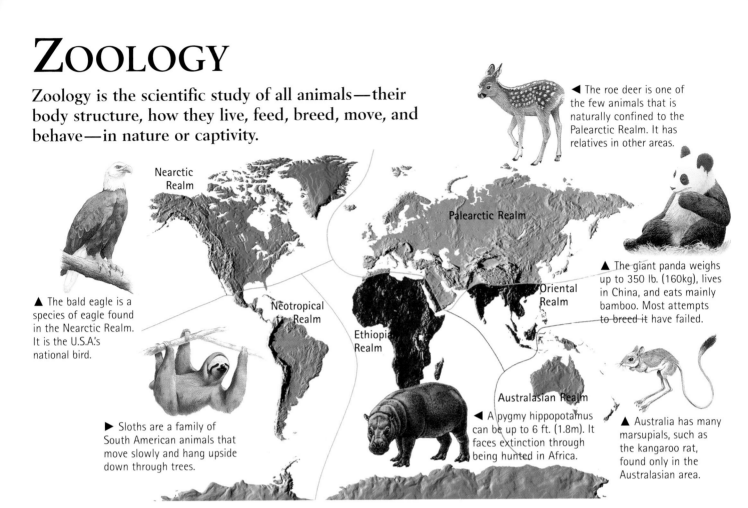

▲ The roe deer is one of the few animals that is naturally confined to the Palearctic Realm. It has relatives in other areas.

▲ The bald eagle is a species of eagle found in the Nearctic Realm. It is the U.S.A.'s national bird.

▲ The giant panda weighs up to 350 lb. (160kg), lives in China, and eats mainly bamboo. Most attempts to breed it have failed.

▶ Sloths are a family of South American animals that move slowly and hang upside down through trees.

◀ A pygmy hippopotamus can be up to 6 ft. (1.8m). It faces extinction through being hunted in Africa.

▲ Australia has many marsupials, such as the kangaroo rat, found only in the Australasian area.

Nearctic Realm · Palearctic Realm · Neotropical Realm · Oriental Realm · Ethiopian Realm · Australasian Realm

## GROUPING ANIMALS

Zoologists divide the Earth into six distinct regions, or realms, following the work, in the 1800s, of British wildlife expert, Alfred Russel Wallace. He first noticed that whole orders or families of animals, birds, and freshwater fish may be confined to one region. This map shows the six realms and an example of the animals found only in each area.

The animal kingdom is vast, varied, and complicated. Zoology has many specialist branches. These often overlap. Some branches deal with particular groups of animals. For example, entomology is the detailed study of insects. Ichthyology specializes in fish. Herpetology is the study of amphibians and reptiles.

## LEARNING ABOUT ANIMALS

Other branches of zoology deal with the features that animals share. Anatomists study the structure of an animal's body and the parts inside, such as the heart, nerves, intestines, and kidneys. Physiologists look at how these parts work, for example how worms take food from soil or how fish take in oxygen through gills. Embryologists deal with development of animals before birth.

## THE LIVING AND THE DEAD

Some areas of zoology are very wide-ranging. Ethologists watch animal behavior—their actions and instincts. Ecologists study how a creature fits into its surroundings or habitat. They observe its needs, such as food and shelter, and its predators. Paleontologists study fossil remains that tell us about prehistoric life, such as dinosaurs. They deal with dead remains, but still need a good knowledge of living animals to reconstruct finds and compare them with other creatures.

## WHAT ZOOLOGISTS DO

Some zoologists are desk-based, writing reports or books. Others work in laboratories, carrying out tests and experiments. Some are based in museums, zoos, or wildlife parks, and others are in the field—watching, taking notes on, and photographing animals in the wild. Many deal with the media: for example, campaigning to save endangered creatures or giving pet advice.

▼ A keeper at Marwell Zoo (U.K.) bottle-feeds a baby okapi, a very rare African animal. Breeding threatened species such as this is one invaluable role of a zoo. Many breed animals in captivity to help boost their dwindling numbers in the wild.

## SEE ALSO

Animal, Conservation, Evolution, Mammal, Prehistoric animal

Propelled by rocket engines, the supersonic X-15 holds the world air-speed record at 4,520 mph set in 1967.

The funeral mask of the pharaoh Tutankhamen was found in his tomb, discovered in 1922.

The first washing machine (invented by Hamilton Smith, U.S.A., 1858) still relied on muscle power.

On April 12, 1961, Yuri Gagarin of the U.S.S.R. became the first person in space onboard *Vostok 1*.

The steam gun carriage of 1769, invented by French engineer Cugnot, was the first motorized vehicle.

# FACTFINDER

Whether for school projects, or just for fun, this section provides facts, figures, and other essential information—from a world map to presidents and states, and on to biographies of famous figures. It finishes with the highlights of the 20th century. Timelines present key international (top) and U.S. (bottom) developments.

The *chanoyu*, a Japanese tea ceremony which can last four hours, actually originated in China.

In 1834, Charles Babbage (1792-1871) designed the first mechanical computer, but he never saw it built.

The Venus flytrap is a carnivorous plant that feeds on the insects it traps in its leaves.

U.S. astronauts use a Manned Maneuvering Unit (MMU) to guide themselves when floating free in space. This contains several small rocket thrusters pointing in different directions. When one is fired, the astronaut moves in the opposite direction.

The Arctic tern is a long-distance flyer, making an annual round trip of up to 25,000 miles.

*Camptosaurus* was an ornithopod ("bird-footed") dinosaur that lived about 150 million years ago.

Edgar Allan Poe (1809-49) was one of America's greatest poets and an early writer of horror stories.

# COUNTRIES OF THE WORLD

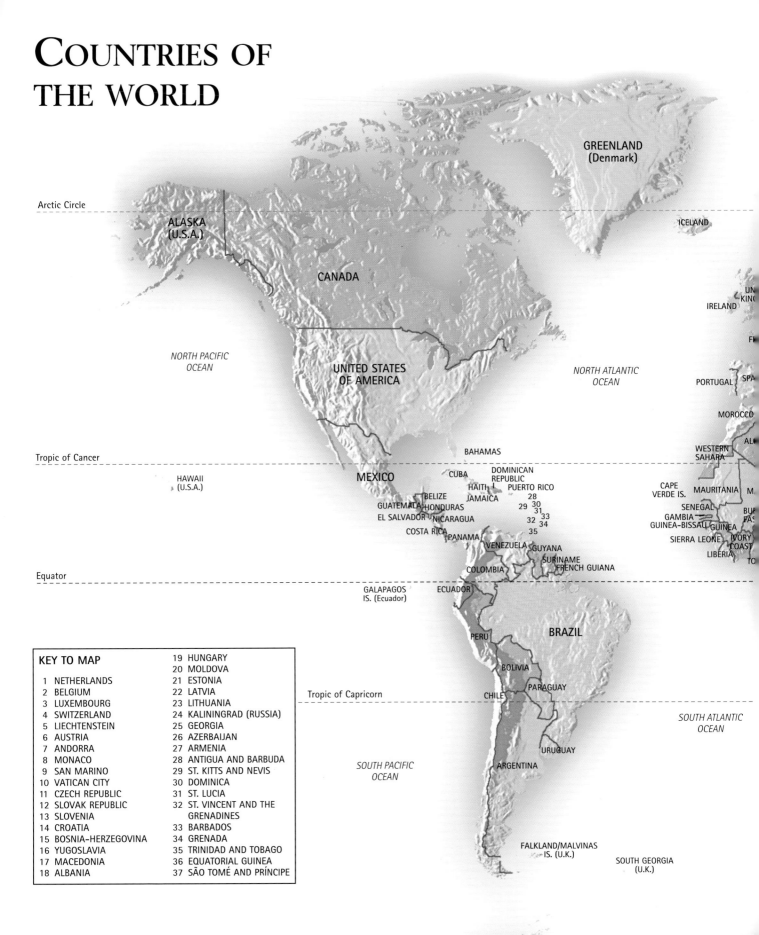

Arctic Circle

GREENLAND
(Denmark)

ALASKA
(U.S.A.)

ICELAND

CANADA

UN
KING

IRELAND

NORTH PACIFIC
OCEAN

NORTH ATLANTIC
OCEAN

F

UNITED STATES
OF AMERICA

PORTUGAL    SPA

MOROCCO

Tropic of Cancer

WESTERN
SAHARA

AL

BAHAMAS

HAWAII
(U.S.A.)

MEXICO

CUBA

DOMINICAN
REPUBLIC

HAITI    PUERTO RICO

CAPE
VERDE IS.    MAURITANIA    M.

BELIZE        JAMAICA        28
GUATEMALA HONDURAS            29  30
                                   31
EL SALVADOR  NICARAGUA        32    33
                                     34
COSTA RICA        35
        PANAMA

SENEGAL
GAMBIA                        BU
GUINEA-BISSAU  GUINEA    FAS

SIERRA LEONE    IVORY
                COAST
            LIBERIA      TO

VENEZUELA  GUYANA
         SURINAME
COLOMBIA      FRENCH GUIANA

Equator

GALAPAGOS
IS. (Ecuador)

ECUADOR

PERU

BRAZIL

## KEY TO MAP

| | |
|---|---|
| | 19  HUNGARY |
| | 20  MOLDOVA |
| 1  NETHERLANDS | 21  ESTONIA |
| 2  BELGIUM | 22  LATVIA |
| 3  LUXEMBOURG | 23  LITHUANIA |
| 4  SWITZERLAND | 24  KALININGRAD (RUSSIA) |
| 5  LIECHTENSTEIN | 25  GEORGIA |
| 6  AUSTRIA | 26  AZERBAIJAN |
| 7  ANDORRA | 27  ARMENIA |
| 8  MONACO | 28  ANTIGUA AND BARBUDA |
| 9  SAN MARINO | 29  ST. KITTS AND NEVIS |
| 10  VATICAN CITY | 30  DOMINICA |
| 11  CZECH REPUBLIC | 31  ST. LUCIA |
| 12  SLOVAK REPUBLIC | 32  ST. VINCENT AND THE |
| 13  SLOVENIA |       GRENADINES |
| 14  CROATIA | 33  BARBADOS |
| 15  BOSNIA-HERZEGOVINA | 34  GRENADA |
| 16  YUGOSLAVIA | 35  TRINIDAD AND TOBAGO |
| 17  MACEDONIA | 36  EQUATORIAL GUINEA |
| 18  ALBANIA | 37  SÃO TOMÉ AND PRÍNCIPE |

BOLIVIA

Tropic of Capricorn

CHILE

PARAGUAY

SOUTH ATLANTIC
OCEAN

SOUTH PACIFIC
OCEAN

URUGUAY

ARGENTINA

FALKLAND/MALVINAS
IS. (U.K.)

SOUTH GEORGIA
(U.K.)

Antarctic Circle

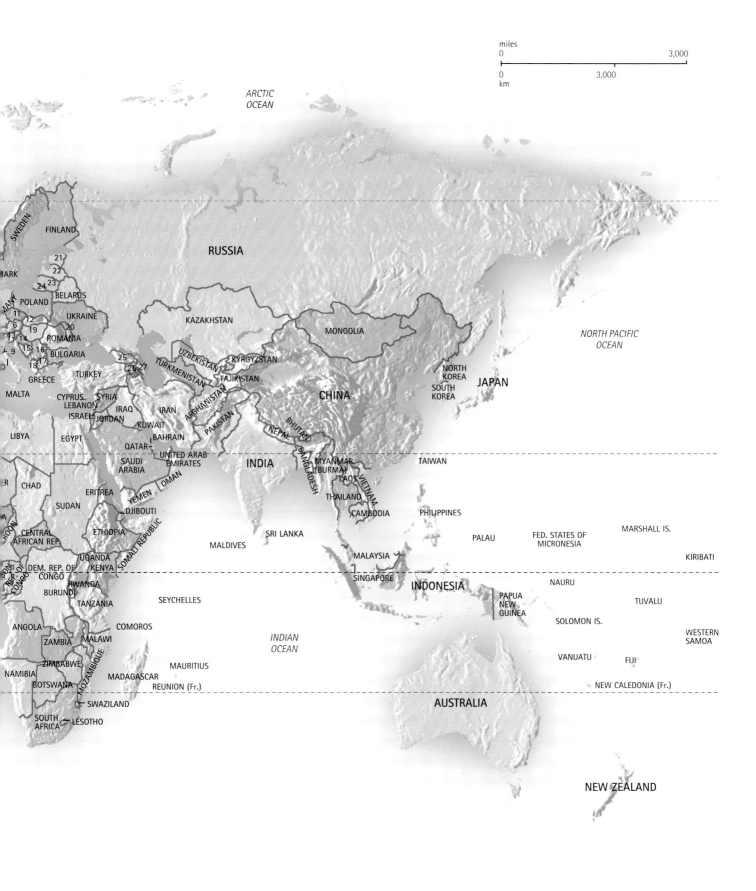

miles
0                                           3,000

0                          3,000
km

ARCTIC
OCEAN

SWEDEN
FINLAND

RUSSIA

21

MARK          22
        24 23
          BELARUS
GANY  POLAND
11      UKRAINE
6   12                    KAZAKHSTAN          MONGOLIA
19      20
13 14  ROMANIA
9                                  KYRGYZSTAN
15 16  BULGARIA              UZBEKISTAN
18  17              25
    GREECE  TURKEY    26 27  TURKMENISTAN        NORTH
                          TAJIKISTAN            KOREA        JAPAN
MALTA                                                  SOUTH
    CYPRUS  SYRIA          AFGHANISTAN    CHINA      KOREA
    LEBANON                                
    ISRAEL  IRAQ  IRAN                              
LIBYA        JORDAN  KUWAIT    PAKISTAN        BHUTAN
    EGYPT          BAHRAIN          NEPAL
              QATAR            BANGLADESH  MYANMAR              TAIWAN
        SAUDI  UNITED ARAB    INDIA        (BURMA)
ER  CHAD  ARABIA  EMIRATES            LAOS  VIETNAM
                OMAN                          
        ERITREA            YEMEN            THAILAND
    SUDAN                              CAMBODIA      PHILIPPINES
            DJIBOUTI                                
OON  CENTRAL  ETHIOPIA              SRI LANKA                      MARSHALL IS.
    AFRICAN REP.                  MALDIVES            PALAU  FED. STATES OF
                SOMALI REPUBLIC                            MICRONESIA
OF  DEM. REP. OF  UGANDA                        MALAYSIA                      KIRIBATI
CONGO    KENYA                                      
CONGO  RWANDA                          SINGAPORE            NAURU
    BURUNDI                                      INDONESIA
        TANZANIA        SEYCHELLES                        PAPUA            TUVALU
                                              NEW
ANGOLA                                        GUINEA
    ZAMBIA  MALAWI                  INDIAN              SOLOMON IS.      WESTERN
    ZIMBABWE                      OCEAN                                SAMOA
                    COMOROS                              VANUATU    FIJI
NAMIBIA            MAURITIUS                      
    BOTSWANA  MADAGASCAR                            NEW CALEDONIA (Fr.)
            REUNION (Fr.)
        SWAZILAND                                      AUSTRALIA
SOUTH    LESOTHO
AFRICA

NORTH PACIFIC
OCEAN

NEW ZEALAND

ANTARCTICA

# STATES OF THE UNITED STATES

| STATE | CAPITAL | POPULATION (1997 ESTIMATE) | (RANK) | AREA (IN SQ. MI.) | (RANK) | ENTRY INTO UNION | (ORDER) |
|---|---|---|---|---|---|---|---|
| Alabama | Montgomery | 4,319,000 | (23) | 52,423 | (30) | December 14, 1819 | (22) |
| Alaska | Juneau | 609,000 | (48) | 656,424 | (1) | January 3, 1959 | (49) |
| Arizona | Phoenix | 4,555,000 | (21) | 114,006 | (6) | February 14, 1912 | (48) |
| Arkansas | Little Rock | 2,523,000 | (33) | 53,182 | (29) | June 15, 1836 | (25) |
| California | Sacramento | 32,268,000 | (1) | 163,707 | (3) | September 9, 1850 | (31) |
| Colorado | Denver | 3,893,000 | (25) | 104,100 | (8) | August 1, 1876 | (38) |
| Connecticut | Hartford | 3270,000 | (28) | 5,544 | (48) | January 9, 1788 | (5) |
| Delaware | Dover | 732,000 | (46) | 2,489 | (49) | December 7, 1787 | (1) |
| Florida | Tallahassee | 14,654,000 | (4) | 65,758 | (22) | March 3, 1845 | (27) |
| Georgia | Atlanta | 7,486,000 | (10) | 59,441 | (24) | January 2, 1788 | (4) |
| Hawaii | Honolulu | 1,187,000 | (41) | 10,932 | (43) | August 21, 1959 | (50) |
| Idaho | Boise | 1,210,000 | (40) | 83,574 | (14) | July 3, 1890 | (43) |
| Illinois | Springfield | 11,896,000 | (6) | 57,918 | (25) | December 3, 1818 | (21) |
| Indiana | Indianapolis | 5,864,000 | (14) | 36,420 | (38) | December 11, 1816 | (19) |
| Iowa | Des Moines | 2,852,000 | (30) | 56,276 | (26) | December 28, 1846 | (29) |
| Kansas | Topeka | 2,595,000 | (32) | 82,282 | (15) | January 29, 1861 | (34) |
| Kentucky | Frankfort | 3,908,000 | (24) | 40,411 | (37) | June 1, 1792 | (15) |
| Louisiana | Baton Rouge | 4,352,000 | (22) | 51,843 | (31) | April 30, 1812 | (18) |
| Maine | Augusta | 1,242,000 | (39) | 35,387 | (39) | March 15, 1820 | (23) |
| Maryland | Annapolis | 5,094,000 | (19) | 12,407 | (42) | April 28, 1788 | (7) |
| Massachusetts | Boston | 6,118,000 | (13) | 10,555 | (44) | February 6, 1788 | (6) |
| Michigan | Lansing | 9,774,000 | (8) | 96,705 | (11) | January 26, 1837 | (26) |
| Minnesota | St. Paul | 4,686,000 | (20) | 86,943 | (12) | May 11, 1858 | (32) |
| Mississippi | Jackson | 2,731,000 | (31) | 48,434 | (32) | December 10, 1817 | (20) |
| Missouri | Jefferson City | 5,402,000 | (16) | 69,709 | (21) | August 10, 1821 | (24) |
| Montana | Helena | 879,000 | (44) | 147,046 | (4) | November 8, 1889 | (41) |
| Nebraska | Lincoln | 1,657,000 | (38) | 77,358 | (16) | March 1, 1867 | (37) |
| Nevada | Carson City | 1,677,000 | (37) | 110,567 | (7) | October 31, 1864 | (36) |
| New Hampshire | Concord | 1,173,000 | (42) | 9,351 | (46) | June 21, 1788 | (9) |
| New Jersey | Trenton | 8,053,000 | (9) | 8,722 | (47) | December 18, 1787 | (3) |
| New Mexico | Santa Fe | 1,730,000 | (36) | 121,598 | (5) | January 6, 1912 | (47) |
| New York | Albany | 18,137,000 | (3) | 54,556 | (27) | July 26, 1788 | (11) |
| North Carolina | Raleigh | 7,425,000 | (11) | 53,821 | (28) | November 21, 1789 | (12) |
| North Dakota | Bismarck | 641,000 | (47) | 70,704 | (19) | November 2, 1889 | (39) |
| Ohio | Columbus | 11,186,000 | (7) | 44,828 | (34) | March 1, 1803 | (17) |
| Oklahoma | Oklahoma City | 3,317,000 | (27) | 69,903 | (20) | November 16, 1907 | (46) |
| Oregon | Salem | 3,243,000 | (29) | 98,386 | (9) | February 14, 1859 | (33) |
| Pennsylvania | Harrisburg | 12,020,000 | (5) | 46,058 | (33) | December 12, 1787 | (2) |
| Rhode Island | Providence | 987,000 | (43) | 1,545 | (50) | May 29, 1790 | (13) |
| South Carolina | Columbia | 3,760,000 | (26) | 32,008 | (40) | May 23, 1788 | (8) |
| South Dakota | Pierre | 738,000 | (45) | 77,121 | (17) | November 2, 1889 | (40) |
| Tennessee | Nashville | 5,368,000 | (17) | 42,146 | (36) | June 1, 1796 | (16) |
| Texas | Austin | 19,439,000 | (2) | 268,601 | (2) | December 29, 1845 | (28) |
| Utah | Salt Lake City | 2,059,000 | (34) | 84,904 | (13) | January 4, 1896 | (45) |
| Vermont | Montpelier | 589,000 | (49) | 9,615 | (45) | March 4, 1791 | (14) |
| Virginia | Richmond | 6,734,000 | (12) | 42,777 | (35) | June 25, 1788 | (10) |
| Washington | Olympia | 5,610,000 | (15) | 71,302 | (18) | November 11, 1889 | (42) |
| West Virginia | Charleston | 1,816,000 | (35) | 24,231 | (41) | June 20, 1863 | (35) |
| Wisconsin | Madison | 5,170,000 | (18) | 65,499 | (23) | May 29, 1848 | (30) |
| Wyoming | Cheyenne | 480,000 | (50) | 97,818 | (10) | July 10, 1890 | (44) |

# PRESIDENTS OF THE UNITED STATES

| NAME (PARTY)* | BIRTH-DEATH DATES | TERM IN OFFICE | VICE PRESIDENT(S) |
|---|---|---|---|
| 1. George Washington (F) | 1732 – 1799 | Apr. 30, 1789 – Mar. 4, 1797 | John Adams |
| 2. John Adams (F) | 1735 – 1826 | Mar. 4, 1797 – Mar. 4, 1801 | Thomas Jefferson |
| 3. Thomas Jefferson (D–R) | 1743 – 1826 | Mar. 4, 1801 – Mar. 4, 1809 | Aaron Burr<br>George Clinton |
| 4. James Madison (D–R) | 1751 – 1836 | Mar. 4, 1809 – Mar. 4, 1817 | George Clinton<br>Elbridge Gerry |
| 5. James Monroe (D–R) | 1758 – 1831 | Mar. 4, 1817 – Mar. 4, 1825 | Daniel D. Tompkins |
| 6. John Quincy Adams (D–R) | 1767 – 1848 | Mar. 4, 1825 – Mar. 4, 1829 | John C. Calhoun |
| 7. Andrew Jackson (D) | 1767 – 1845 | Mar. 4, 1829 – Mar. 4, 1837 | John C. Calhoun,<br>Martin Van Buren |
| 8. Martin Van Buren (D) | 1782 – 1862 | Mar. 4, 1837 – Mar. 4, 1841 | Richard M. Johnson |
| 9. William Henry Harrison (W) | 1773 – 1841 | Mar. 4, 1841 – Apr. 4, 1841 | John Tyler |
| 10. John Tyler (W) | 1790 – 1862 | Apr. 4, 1841 – Mar. 4, 1845 | – |
| 11. James K. Polk (D) | 1795 – 1849 | Mar. 4, 1845 – Mar. 4, 1849 | George M. Dallas |
| 12. Zachary Taylor (W) | 1784 – 1850 | Mar. 4, 1849 – July 9, 1850 | Millard Fillmore |
| 13. Millard Fillmore (W) | 1800 – 1874 | July 9, 1850 – Mar. 4, 1853 | – |
| 14. Franklin Pierce (D) | 1804 – 1869 | Mar. 4, 1853 – Mar. 4, 1857 | William R. King |
| 15. James Buchanan (D) | 1791 – 1868 | Mar. 4, 1857 – Mar. 4, 1861 | John C. Breckinridge |
| 16. Abraham Lincoln (R) | 1809 – 1865 | Mar. 4, 1861 – Apr. 15, 1865 | Hannibal Hamlin,<br>Andrew Johnson |
| 17. Andrew Johnson (R) | 1808 – 1875 | Apr. 15, 1865 – Mar. 4, 1869 | – |
| 18. Ulysses S. Grant (R) | 1822 – 1885 | Mar. 4, 1869 – Mar. 4, 1877 | Schuyler Colfax<br>Henry Wilson |
| 19. Rutherford B. Hayes (R) | 1822 – 1893 | Mar. 4, 1877 – Mar. 4, 1881 | William A. Wheeler |
| 20. James A. Garfield (R) | 1831 – 1881 | Mar. 4, 1881 – Sept. 19, 1881 | Chester A. Arthur |
| 21. Chester A. Arthur (R) | 1829 – 1886 | Sept. 19, 1881 – Mar. 4, 1885 | – |
| 22. Grover Cleveland (D) | 1837 – 1908 | Mar. 4, 1885 – Mar. 4, 1889 | Thomas A. Hendricks |
| 23. Benjamin Harrison (R) | 1833 – 1901 | Mar. 4, 1889 – Mar. 4, 1893 | Levi P. Morton |
| 24. Grover Cleveland (D) | 1837 – 1908 | Mar. 4, 1893 – Mar. 4, 1897 | Adlai E. Stevenson |
| 25. William McKinley (R) | 1843 – 1901 | Mar. 4, 1897 – Sept. 14, 1901 | Garret A. Hobart<br>Theodore Roosevelt |
| 26. Theodore Roosevelt (R) | 1858 – 1919 | Sept. 14, 1901 – Mar. 4, 1909 | Charles W. Fairbanks |
| 27. William H. Taft (R) | 1857 – 1930 | Mar. 4, 1909 – Mar. 4, 1913 | James S. Sherman |
| 28. Woodrow Wilson (D) | 1856 – 1924 | Mar. 4, 1913 – Mar. 4, 1921 | Thomas R. Marshall |
| 29. Warren G. Harding (R) | 1865 – 1923 | Mar. 4, 1921 – Aug. 2, 1923 | Calvin Coolidge |
| 30. Calvin Coolidge (R) | 1872 – 1933 | Aug. 3, 1923 – Mar. 4, 1929 | Charles G. Dawes |
| 31. Herbert Hoover (R) | 1874 – 1964 | Mar. 4, 1929 – Mar. 4, 1933 | Charles Curtis |
| 32. Franklin D. Roosevelt (D) | 1882 – 1945 | Mar. 4, 1933 – Apr. 12, 1945 | John N. Garner<br>Henry A. Wallace<br>Harry S. Truman |
| 33. Harry S. Truman (D) | 1884 – 1972 | Apr. 12, 1945 – Jan. 20, 1953 | Alben W. Barkley |
| 34. Dwight D. Eisenhower (R) | 1890 – 1969 | Jan. 20, 1953 – Jan. 20, 1961 | Richard M. Nixon |
| 35. John F. Kennedy (D) | 1917 – 1963 | Jan. 20, 1961 – Nov. 22, 1963 | Lyndon B. Johnson |
| 36. Lyndon B. Johnson (D) | 1908 – 1973 | Nov. 22, 1963 – Jan. 20, 1969 | Hubert H. Humphrey |
| 37. Richard M. Nixon (R) | 1913 – 1994 | Jan. 20, 1969 – Aug. 9, 1974 | Spiro T. Agnew<br>Gerald R. Ford |
| 38. Gerald R. Ford (R) | 1913 – | Aug. 9, 1974 – Jan. 20, 1977 | Nelson A. Rockefeller |
| 39. Jimmy Carter (D) | 1924 – | Jan. 20, 1977 – Jan. 20, 1981 | Walter F. Mondale |
| 40. Ronald Reagan (R) | 1911 – | Jan. 20, 1981 – Jan. 20, 1989 | George Bush |
| 41. George Bush (R) | 1924 – | Jan. 20, 1989 – Jan. 20, 1993 | Dan Quayle |
| 42. Bill Clinton (D) | 1946 – | Jan. 20, 1993 – | Al Gore |

*Federalist (F), Whig (W), Democratic–Republican (D–R), Republican (R), Democrat (D)

George Washington refused a third term as the first U.S. President.

Abraham Lincoln was the first president assassinated in office.

Franklin D. Roosevelt led the U.S. during the Depression and WWII.

John F. Kennedy symbolized the young spirit of the 1960s.

The Statue of Liberty welcomes all who enter New York Harbor.

Sir John A. MacDonald led the first government of Canada as a Dominion.

## POPULATION OF LARGEST AMERICAN CITIES (1996 estimate)

| RANK | CITY | POPULATION | RANK | CITY | POPULATION | RANK | CITY | POPULATION |
|---|---|---|---|---|---|---|---|---|
| 1. | New York City, NY | 7,380,906 | 26. | Denver, CO | 497,840 | 51. | Mesa, AZ | 344,764 |
| 2. | Los Angeles, CA | 3,553,638 | 27. | Portland, OR | 480,824 | 52. | Wichita, KS | 320,395 |
| 3. | Chicago, IL | 2,721,547 | 28. | Fort Worth, TX | 479,716 | 53. | Toledo, OH | 317,606 |
| 4. | Houston, TX | 1,744,058 | 29. | New Orleans, LA | 476,625 | 54. | Buffalo, NY | 310,548 |
| 5. | Philadelphia, PA | 1,478,002 | 30. | Oklahoma City, OK | 469,852 | 55. | Santa Ana, CA | 302,419 |
| 6. | San Diego, CA | 1,171,121 | 31. | Tucson, AZ | 449,002 | 56. | Arlington, TX | 294,816 |
| 7. | Phoenix, AZ | 1,159,014 | 32. | Charlotte, NC | 441,297 | 57. | Anaheim, CA | 288,945 |
| 8. | San Antonio, TX | 1,067,816 | 33. | Kansas City, MO | 441,259 | 58. | Tampa, FL | 285,206 |
| 9. | Dallas, TX | 1,053,292 | 34. | Virginia Beach, VA | 430,385 | 59. | Corpus Christi, TX | 280,260 |
| 10. | Detroit, MI | 1,000,272 | 35. | Honolulu, HI | 423,475 | 60. | Newark, NJ | 268,510 |
| 11. | San Jose, CA | 838,744 | 36. | Long Beach, CA | 421,904 | 61. | Louisville, KY | 260,689 |
| 12. | Indianapolis, IN | 746,737 | 37. | Albuquerque, NM | 419,681 | 62. | St. Paul, MN | 259,606 |
| 13. | San Francisco, CA | 735,315 | 38. | Atlanta, GA | 401,907 | 63. | Birmingham, AL | 258,543 |
| 14. | Jacksonville, FL | 679,792 | 39. | Fresno, CA | 396,011 | 64. | Riverside, CA | 255,069 |
| 15. | Baltimore, MD | 675,401 | 40. | Tulsa, OK | 378,491 | 65. | Aurora, CO | 252,341 |
| 16. | Columbus, OH | 657,053 | 41. | Las Vegas, NV | 376,906 | 66. | Anchorage, AK | 250,505 |
| 17. | El Paso, TX | 599,865 | 42. | Sacramento, CA | 376,243 | 67. | Raleigh, NC | 243,835 |
| 18. | Memphis, TN | 596,725 | 43. | Oakland, CA | 367,230 | 68. | Lexington-Fayette, KY | 239,942 |
| 19. | Milwaukee, WI | 590,503 | 44. | Miami, FL | 365,127 | 69. | St. Petersburg, FL | 235,988 |
| 20. | Boston, MA | 558,394 | 45. | Omaha, NE | 364,253 | 70. | Norfolk, VA | 233,430 |
| 21. | Washington, DC | 543,213 | 46. | Minneapolis, MN | 358,785 | 71. | Stockton, CA | 232,660 |
| 22. | Austin, TX | 541,278 | 47. | St. Louis, MO | 351,565 | 72. | Jersey City, NJ | 229,039 |
| 23. | Seattle, WA | 524,704 | 48. | Pittsburgh, PA | 350,363 | 73. | Rochester, NY | 221,594 |
| 24. | Nashville-Davidson, TN | 511,263 | 49. | Cincinnati, OH | 345,818 | 74. | Akron, OH | 216,882 |
| 25. | Cleveland, OH | 498,246 | 50. | Colorado Springs, CO | 345,127 | 75. | Baton Rouge, LA | 215,882 |

## THE PROVINCES AND TERRITORIES OF CANADA

| PROVINCES | CAPITAL | POPULATION (1996 CENSUS) | (RANK) | AREA IN SQ. MI. | (RANK) | DATE BECAME PROVINCE |
|---|---|---|---|---|---|---|
| Alberta | Edmonton | 2,696,826 | (4) | 255,287 | (4) | 1905 |
| British Columbia | Victoria | 3,724,500 | (3) | 365,900 | (3) | 1871 |
| Manitoba | Winnipeg | 1,113,898 | (5) | 250,947 | (6) | 1870 |
| New Brunswick | Fredericton | 738,133 | (8) | 28,355 | (8) | 1867 |
| Newfoundland | St. John's | 551,792 | (9) | 156,649 | (7) | 1949 |
| Nova Scotia | Halifax | 909,282 | (7) | 21,425 | (9) | 1867 |
| Ontario | Toronto | 10,753,573 | (1) | 412,581 | (2) | 1867 |
| Prince Edward Island | Charlottetown | 134,557 | (10) | 2,185 | (10) | 1873 |
| Quebec | Quebec | 7,138,795 | (2) | 594,860 | (1) | 1867 |
| Saskatchewan | Regina | 990,237 | (6) | 251,866 | (5) | 1905 |

| TERRITORIES | CAPITAL | POPULATION (1996 CENSUS) | AREA IN SQ. MI. |
|---|---|---|---|
| Northwest Territories | Yellowknife | 64,402 | 1,322,910 |
| Yukon Territory | Whitehorse | 30,766 | 186,661 |

## PRIME MINISTERS OF CANADA

| NAME | SERVED | POLITCAL PARTY |
|---|---|---|
| Sir John A. Macdonald | 1867–1873 | Conservative |
| Alexander Mackenzie | 1873–1878 | Liberal |
| Sir John A. Macdonald | 1878–1891 | Convervative |
| Sir John Abbott | 1891–1892 | Conservative |
| Sir John Thompson | 1892–1894 | Conservative |
| Sir Mackenzie Bowell | 1894–1896 | Conservative |
| Sir Charles Tupper | 1896 | Conservative |
| Sir Wilfrid Laurier | 1896–1911 | Liberal |
| Sir Robert Borden | 1911–1917 | Conservative |
| Sir Robert Borden | 1917–1920 | Unionist |
| Arthur Meighen | 1920–1921 | Unionist |
| W.L. Mackenzie King | 1921–1926 | Liberal |
| Arthur Meighen | 1926 | Conservative |
| W.L. Mackenzie King | 1926–1930 | Liberal |
| Richard Bennett | 1930–1935 | Conservative |
| W.L. Mackenzie King | 1935–1948 | Liberal |
| Louis St. Laurent | 1948–1957 | Liberal |
| John Diefenbaker | 1957–1963 | Progressive Conservative |
| Lester B. Pearson | 1963–1968 | Liberal |
| Pierre E. Trudeau | 1968–1979 | Liberal |
| Charles Joseph Clark | 1979–1980 | Progressive Conservative |
| Pierre E. Trudeau | 1980–1984 | Liberal |
| John Turner | 1984 | Liberal |
| Brian Mulroney | 1984–1993 | Progressive Conservative |
| Kim Campbell | 1993 | Progressive Conservative |
| Jean Chrétien | 1993– | Liberal |

# INTERNATIONAL ORGANIZATIONS

## United Nations (UN)

was founded in 1945. Its goals are to maintain international peace and security, and solve cultural, social, and humanitarian problems. There were 51 original members of the UN; in 1997 there were 185 members. Headquarters: New York City. The UN's main organs include: the General Assembly, with representatives of all members; the Security Council, with 15 members, 5 of whom (China, France, Russia, U.K., and U.S.) have permanent seats and 10 of whom are elected for 2 years; and the International Court of Justice, or World Court, which sits in The Hague, Netherlands.

*Following are eight of the UN's specialized and related agencies:*

## Food and Agriculture Organization (FAO)

helps improve production and distribution of food and world dietary standards. Headquarters: Rome, Italy.

## International Bank for Reconstruction and Development (IBRD),

or World Bank, provides loans and technical help for economic projects in developing countries. Headquarters: Washington, D.C.

## International Monetary Fund (IMF)

promotes monetary cooperation and the expansion of world trade. Headquarters: Washington, D.C.

## United Nations Children's Fund (UNICEF)

helps children in developing nations. Headquarters: New York City.

## United Nations Educational, Scientific, and Cultural Organization (UNESCO)

promotes exchange of information, ideas, and culture. Headquarters: Paris, France.

## United Nations High Commissioner for Refugees (UNHCR)

provides assistance to refugees worldwide. It is based in Geneva, Switzerland.

## World Health Organization (WHO)

fights disease and helps improve health standards. Headquarters: Geneva, Switzerland.

## World Trade Organization (WTO)

administers trade agreements and attempts to settle disputes. Headquarters: Geneva, Switzerland.

*Other international organizations include:*

## Caribbean Community and Common Market (CARICOM)

was founded in 1973. Members are Antigua and Barbuda, Bahamas, Barbados, Belize, Dominica, Grenada, Guyana, Jamaica, Montserrat, St. Kitts and Nevis, St. Lucia, St. Vincent and the Grenadines, Suriname, and Trinidad and Tobago. Headquarters: Georgetown, Guyana.

## The Commonwealth,

founded in 1949, is a loose association of Great Britain and more than 50 other nations that were once part of the British Empire. Mozambique, the most recent member, had not been part of the British Empire. Headquarters: London, England.

## Commonwealth of Independent States (CIS),

founded in 1991, is made up of 12 of the 15 former Soviet republics. Members are Armenia, Azerbaijan, Belarus, Georgia, Kazakhstan, Kyrgyzstan, Moldova, Russia, Tajikistan, Turkmenistan, Ukraine, and Uzbekistan. Headquarters: Minsk, Belarus.

## European Union (EU),

founded in 1952 with 6 members, was originally a free-trade and customs union. It is now a closer political and economic union. Members are Austria, Belgium, Denmark, Finland, France, Germany, Greece, Ireland, Italy, Luxembourg, the Netherlands, Portugal, Spain, Sweden, and the U.K.

## Group of Eight (G-8),

is a group of eight leading industrialized nations that meet to discuss economic issues. Until Russia was admitted in 1997, it was known as the Group of Seven (G-7). The original members are Canada, France, Germany, Japan, Italy, the U.K., and the U.S.

## International Criminal Police Organization (Interpol),

founded in 1956, promotes cooperation between police authorities in 177 countries. Headquarters: Lyon, France.

## League of Arab States,

also known as the Arab League; promotes economic, social, political, and military cooperation among members. Founded in 1945, it has 22 members, including Palestine, which it considers an independent nation. Headquarters: Cairo, Egypt.

## North Atlantic Treaty Organization (NATO)

is a military alliance of Western nations. It was founded in 1949 to defend Western Europe, the U.S., and Canada from military aggression. Members are Belgium, Canada, Denmark, France, Germany, Greece, Iceland, Italy, Luxembourg, the Netherlands, Norway, Portugal, Spain, Turkey, the U.K., and the U.S. Beginning in 1997, plans were made to admit some former Eastern European communist nations into NATO. Headquarters: Brussels, Belgium.

## Organization for Economic Cooperation and Development (OECD)

was founded in 1961. Its goals are to promote economic growth, financial stability, and social welfare in its 29 member nations and to assist developing nations. Headquarters: Paris, France.

## Organization of African Unity (OAU)

was founded in 1963 to promote unity and cooperation among African nations. It has 53 members. Headquarters: Addis Ababa, Ethiopia.

## Organization of American States (OAS)

was founded in 1948. Its major goal is the peaceful settlement of disputes between nations. It has 35 members. Cuba has been suspended from OAS activities since 1962, but not from membership. Headquarters: Washington, D.C.

## Organization of Petroleum Exporting Countries (OPEC)

was founded in 1960 to coordinate oil production and prices. Members are Algeria, Indonesia, Iran, Iraq, Kuwait, Libya, Nigeria, Qatar, Saudi Arabia, United Arab Emirates, and Venezuela. Headquarters: Vienna, Austria.

Logo for the League of Arab States, which mediates disputes among its member nations.

Logo for the European Union. This was known as the European Community (EC) until 1994.

The Commonwealth of Independent States is not in itself a state but an alliance of fully independent states.

Since the end of the Cold War in the 1990s, NATO has had to reassess its military role.

| 1618–48 | 1644 | 1700s–1800s | 1756–63 | 1775–83 | 1789–99 | 1804–15 | 1811–25 |

Thirty Years' War | Start of Manchu rule in China | Industrial Revolution | Seven Years' War | Revolutionary War | French Revolution | Napoleonic Wars | Latin American nations win independence

# BIOGRAPHIES

## ARTISTS

Leonardo was not only an artist, but also an inventor, mathematician, engineer, and anatomist.

Picasso was the most famous artist of the 20th century. His work changed the course of modern art.

Chaucer's *Canterbury Tales* is a collection of stories told by pilgrims on their journey to Canterbury.

Brought up in poverty himself, Dickens wrote knowledgeably about the lives of the poor.

**Audubon, John James (1785-1851),** a U.S. artist and naturalist, was noted for his paintings of birds.

**Botticelli, Sandro (c.1445-1510)** was an Italian painter. Works such as *Primavera* (Spring) and the *Birth of Venus* reflect the humanist and classical interests of his time.

**Copley, John Singleton (1738-1815)** is considered the greatest painter of colonial America. He painted portraits of people such as Paul Revere in natural poses.

**Cézanne, Paul (1839-1906),** a French painter, started out as an impressionist. His paintings showed the effects of light on objects rather than the objects themselves. He later painted colorful, more solid forms.

**Degas, Edgar (1834-1917),** a French painter and sculptor, was influenced by impressionism and Japanese woodcuts. He was interested in the human form, and many of his subjects were ballet dancers. His paintings include *The Rehearsal* and *Dance Class.*

**Giotto (c.1266-1337),** an Italian painter, revived the art of painting in the early Renaissance period. He was especially known for his religious frescoes, including *Life of Christ* and the *Last Judgment.*

**Goya y Lucientes, Francisco José de (1746-1828),** a Spaniard, painted realistic portraits and scenes from everyday life, including *The Disasters of War.*

**Hopper, Edward (1882-1967)** painted ordinary American scenes. The people in many of his paintings are often shown as lonely or sad.

**Homer, Winslow (1836-1910)** is considered one of the greatest U.S. artists. His paintings, including *Breezing Up* and *Gulf Stream,* captured the power and beauty of the sea.

**Leonardo da Vinci (1452-1519),** an Italian painter and scientist, was a genius. His greatest works include the *Last Supper* and the *Mona Lisa.*

**Michelangelo (1475-1564),** an Italian painter, sculptor, and architect, created the frescoes on the ceiling of the Sistine Chapel and sculptures of the *Pietà* and *David.*

**Monet, Claude (1840-1926),** a French painter, was one of the creators of the impressionist movement. Among his most famous works are *Impression: Sunrise,* the Rouen Cathedral series, and the Water Lily series.

**Picasso, Pablo (1881-1973),** a Spaniard, is thought by many to be the greatest artist of the 20th century. With Georges Braque, he developed cubism, a style in which forms are broken down into geometric shapes.

**Pollock, Jackson (1912-56),** an American, one of the most influential artists of the 20th century, was an abstract expressionist who made the colors and shapes of his paintings reflect his feelings. Among his works are *Autumn Rhythm.*

**Rembrandt (Harmenszoon van Rijn) (1606-69)** was the greatest of the Dutch old master painters. He did many group portraits and self-portraits. Among his works are *The Night Watch* and *Syndics of the Cloth Guild.*

**Rubens, Peter Paul (1577-1640),** a Flemish painter, master of the baroque style. He painted portraits, landscapes, and religious and historical subjects.

**Turner, Joseph M. W. (1775-1851)** was a British landscape painter. He painted in both watercolors and oils. His atmospheric paintings include *The Fighting Téméraire* and *Old Chain Pier at Brighton.*

**Van Gogh, Vincent (1853-90),** a Dutch painter, was famous for his use of color. His paintings include *Sunflowers* and *Starry Night.*

**Warhol, Andy (1926-87)** was a U.S. pioneer in "pop art." He painted pop culture objects, such as Campbell's soup cans, and comic-strip characters.

**Wren, Sir Christopher (1632-1723)** is considered the greatest English architect. His best-known creation was St. Paul's Cathedral in London.

**Wright, Frank Lloyd (1869-1959),** the greatest U.S. architect of the 20th century, designed such masterpieces as the Falling Water House and the Guggenheim Museum.

## WRITERS

**Alcott, Louisa May (1832-88),** a U.S. author, is best known for the novel *Little Women,* a story about the four March sisters and their family during the Civil War.

**Andersen, Hans Christian (1805-75),** a Danish writer, was one of the world's greatest storytellers. He is best known for his fairy tales, such as "The Emperor's New Clothes," "The Snow Queen," "The Little Mermaid," and "The Ugly Duckling."

**Austen, Jane (1775-1817),** an English novelist, wrote about the middle class of English country life in such novels as *Emma, Pride and Prejudice,* and *Sense and Sensibility.*

**Cervantes, Miguel (1547-1616)** was a Spanish novelist and dramatist. His greatest work, *Don Quixote,* details the life of a poor gentleman who wants to be a knight and do knightly deeds.

**Chaucer, Geoffrey (c.1345-1400)** was an English poet whose most famous work was a group of stories called the *Canterbury Tales.*

**Cooper, James Fenimore (1789-1851)** wrote novels about the American frontier in the 1700s. His most famous book was *The Last of the Mohicans.*

**Dante Alighieri (1265-1321)** was Italy's greatest poet. His most famous work was the *Divine Comedy.*

**Dickens, Charles (1812-70)** was one of England's greatest novelists. Some of his novels, including *Oliver Twist* and *David Copperfield,* drew attention to the plight of the poor and underprivileged.

| Louisiana Purchase doubles size of U.S. | War of 1812 | U.S. defeats Mexico in Mexican War; California Gold Rush begins | North and South fight Civil War | President Abraham Lincoln assassinated; 13th Amendment abolishes slavery |

| 1803 | 1812–15 | 1848 | 1861–65 | 1865 |

**Dickinson, Emily (1830–86)**
was one of the most important U.S. poets of the 1800s. She wrote 1,775 poems, but only a few were published when she was alive.

**Frost, Robert (1874–1963)**
was one of the most important U.S. poets of the 20th century. He wrote about the people and the land of New England. Among his books of poetry are *New Hampshire* and *In the Clearing*.

**Goethe, Johann Wolfgang von (1749–1832)**
was a poet, novelist, and playwright of unequaled importance in German literature. His greatest work was *Faust*.

**Hawthorne, Nathaniel (1804–64)**,
born in Massachusetts, was one of the most important American writers of the 1800s. His greatest novel was *The Scarlet Letter*.

**Henry, O. (1862–1910)**
was one of America's foremost short-story writers. His real name was William Sydney Porter. He wrote more than 300 stories, many with surprise endings. One of his most popular stories is "The Gift of the Magi."

**Keats, John (1795–1821)**,
an English poet, wrote beautiful odes, including "To a Nightingale," "On a Grecian Urn," and "To Autumn."

**Longfellow, Henry Wadsworth (1807–82)**
was a modern language professor and popular poet who wrote poems about American history including such long poems as *The Song of Hiawatha*.

**Melville, Herman (1819–91)**
was one of the great U.S. writers. He used his experiences as a sailor when writing his most popular books, *Moby Dick* and *Typee*.

**Poe, Edgar Allan (1809–49)**,
a U.S. author, has been called the father of modern mystery and horror stories. His short stories include, "The Fall of the House of Usher," and "The Pit and the Pendulum." Poems include "The Raven" and "The Bells."

**Sandburg, Carl (1878–1967)**
was one of the most beloved U.S poets, as well as a biographer. His biography of Abraham Lincoln won the 1940 Pulitzer Prize for history.

**Shakespeare, William (1564–1616)**,
an English dramatist and poet, is considered by many to be the world's greatest writer. His plays include *A Midsummer Night's Dream*, *Hamlet*, and *Macbeth*.

**Stevenson, Robert Louis (1850–94)**
was a versatile Scottish author. He wrote *A Child's Garden of Verses*, and such adventure stories as *Treasure Island* and *Kidnapped*.

**Stowe, Harriet Beecher (1811–96)**,
a U.S. author, was famous for her novel *Uncle Tom's Cabin*. It made a powerful case against slavery.

**Swift, Jonathan (1667–1745)**
was an English writer whose books poked fun at the silly, cruel behavior of people and governments. His most famous book is *Gulliver's Travels*.

**Tolstoy, Count Leo (1828–1910)**
was a Russian novelist. Two of his greatest books were *War and Peace* and *Anna Karenina*.

**Twain, Mark (1835–1910)**
was a popular U.S. novelist and journalist. His real name was Samuel Clemens. Among his bestselling books were *The Adventures of Tom Sawyer* and *The Adventures of Huckleberry Finn*.

**Wordsworth, William (1770–1850)**
was one of England's greatest poets. His poetry explores the lives of ordinary people in contact with nature. Together with his friend Samuel Taylor Coleridge, he wrote the *Lyrical Ballads*, which included his poem "Tintern Abbey."

# COMPOSERS AND MUSICIANS

**Bach, Johann Sebastian (1685–1750)**,
a German, was one of the world's greatest composers. He wrote concertos and sacred cantatas. His masterpieces include the six *Brandenburg Concertos*, *St. Matthew Passion*, and *B Minor Mass*.

**Beethoven, Ludwig van (1770–1827)**,
a German, wrote sonatas, symphonies, choral and chamber music, and concertos. Major works include his Ninth Symphony, the Piano Concerto no. 5, and the opera *Fidelio*.

**Berlin, Irving (1888–1989)**
was one of the greatest U.S. writers of popular music. He wrote nearly 1,000 songs, including "*Alexander's Ragtime Band*," "*This Is the Army*," and "*God Bless America*."

**Bizet, Georges (1838–75)**,
a French composer, is most famous for his opera *Carmen*.

**Brahms, Johannes (1833–97)**,
a German Romantic composer and gifted pianist, wrote piano sonatas, symphonies, and choral works.

**Britten, Benjamin (1913–76)**,
a British composer, wrote such operas as *Billy Budd* and *Death in Venice*. He also wrote large-scale instrumental works, including *The Young Person's Guide to the Orchestra*.

**Copland, Aaron (1900–90)**,
U.S. composer best known for using jazz and American folk tunes in his classical compositions. His works include the music for such ballets as *Billy the Kid*, *Rodeo*, and *Appalachian Spring*.

**Ellington, Duke (1899–1974)**
was the greatest U.S. jazz composer. He wrote more than 2,000 jazz compositions, plus concert works, religious music, and scores for theater, ballet, and film.

**Gershwin, George (1898–1937)**
was one of the most important U.S. songwriters of the 20th century. He produced many concert works and Broadway musicals. Gershwin's best-known works include *Porgy and Bess*, an opera, and *Rhapsody in Blue*, an orchestral work.

**Handel, Georg Frideric (1685–1759)**,
a German-born British composer, was famous for the oratorio *Messiah*. His orchestral works include *Water Music* and *Music for the Royal Fireworks*.

**Haydn, Franz Joseph (1732–1809)**,
an Austrian composer, was the most famous composer of his day, and he is known as the "father of the symphony." His output included 104 symphonies, about 50 concertos, and 84 string quartets, among other works.

**Ives, Charles (1874–1954)**
was one of the most important U.S. composers of the 20th century. His works

Tolstoy introduced a new form of Christianity into Russia, writing religious works as well as novels.

Tom Sawyer's adventures on the Mississippi River were based on Twain's own boyhood experiences.

Beethoven's music is among the greatest in the world and still influences composers today.

Duke Ellington was one of America's best-known jazz band leaders of the 1930s. He wrote over 50 hits.

| 1904–5 | 1912 | 1914–18 | 1917 | 1929 | 1933 | 1936–39 |
|---|---|---|---|---|---|---|
| Russia defeated in Russo–Japanese War | Chinese overthrow Manchu Dynasty; establish republic | World War I | Communists seize power in Russia | Wall Street Crash starts worldwide depression | Hitler comes to power in Germany | Civil war in Spain |

Mozart began writing music at the age of five. Two years later, he was playing in concerts.

Marie and Pierre Curie devoted their lives to research, spending their own money on equipment.

Edison's first phonograph, a recording machine, led to the development of the record player.

Aristotle studied under Plato for 20 years before becoming tutor to Alexander the Great.

included symphonies, sonatas, and orchestral, choral, and chamber music. He also wrote some 150 songs. Many of his compositions used themes from American folk music.

**Monteverdi, Claudio (1567-1643),** an Italian composer, wrote *Orfeo*, which is considered to be the first opera.

**Mozart, Wolfgang Amadeus (1756–91),** an Austrian, was one of the world's greatest composers. He began composing at the age of five and eventually wrote more than 600 pieces of music, including symphonies, piano concertos, and operas such as *Don Giovanni* and *The Marriage of Figaro*.

**Rodgers, Richard (1902–79)** was one of the most successful U.S. composers in the history of entertainment. He wrote the music for such Broadway musicals as *Oklahoma!*, *Pal Joey*, *The King and I*, *South Pacific*, and *The Sound of Music*.

**Sousa, John Philip (1854-1932)** wrote so many U.S. marches he was known as the "March King." His most famous works include "The Stars and Stripes Forever," The Washington Post March," and "Semper Fidelis."

**Stravinsky, Igor (1882-1971),** a Russian-born U.S. composer, wrote symphonies and operas, as well as the music for such ballets as *The Firebird* and *The Rite of Spring*.

**Tchaikovsky, Peter Ilyich (1840-93)** was a Russian composer. He wrote ballet music, symphonies, piano concertos, and operas. Among his best-known works are the ballet *Swan Lake* and his First Piano Concerto.

**Verdi, Giuseppe (1813-1901)** was the leading Italian operatic composer of his day. *Rigoletto*, *La Traviata*, and *Aida* are among his best-known works.

**Vivaldi, Antonio (c.1675-1741)** was a Venetian violinist and composer. He wrote operas, sacred music, and concertos such as *The Four Seasons*.

**Wagner, Richard (1813-83),** a German composer, is best known for his opera cycle *The Ring of the Nibelung*, which consists of four works based on old Germanic mystical legends.

## SCIENTISTS AND INVENTORS

**Bell, Alexander Graham (1847-1922),** a Scottish-born American, invented the telephone.

**Benz, Karl (1844-19129),** a German engineer, built the first practical gasoline-powered automobile.

**Copernicus, Nicolaus (1473-1543),** a Polish astronomer, proved that the Earth moves in orbit around the Sun.

**Curie, Marie (1867-1934),** a Polish physicist, discovered radium, a radioactive substance. She worked with her husband Pierre.

**Daguerre, Louis (1789-1851),** a French painter, invented the first practical photographic process.

**Darwin, Charles (1809-82),** a British naturalist, formulated the theory of evolution by natural selection.

**Edison, Thomas Alva (1847-1931),** a U.S. inventor, patented more than a thousand inventions, including the telegraph and electric lightbulb.

**Einstein, Albert (1879-1955),** a German-born American physicist, changed our view of the universe with his General Theory of Relativity (1915).

**Faraday, Michael (1791-1867),** a British physicist and chemist, was a pioneer in the field of electricity. His work made the dynamo and the electric motor possible.

**Fermi, Enrico (1901-54),** an Italian nuclear physicist, built the first nuclear reactor.

**Fleming, Alexander (1881-1955),** a British bacteriologist, discovered penicillin, the first antibiotic.

**Franklin, Benjamin (1706-90),** a U.S. scientist, publisher, and statesman, proved that lightning is a form of electricity.

**Galilei, Galileo (1564-1642),** an Italian astronomer and physicist, was the first to use the telescope. He also showed that light objects fall as fast as heavy ones when they are pulled toward the Earth by gravity.

**Gutenberg, Johann (c.1400-68),** a German printer, was the first to develop a way to print books with speed and accuracy.

**Harvey, William (1578-1657),** a British physician, discovered that the heart acted as a pump to circulate blood through the body.

**Kepler, Johannes (1571-1630),** a German astronomer, showed that the planets went around the Sun in elliptical paths.

**Marconi, Guglielmo (1874-1937),** an Italian-born British engineer, was the first person to transmit long-distance radio signals.

**Mendel, Gregor (1822-84),** an Austrian priest, biologist, and botanist, researched the laws of heredity using pea plants.

**Morse, Samuel F.B. (1791-1872),** a U.S. inventor, invented the first successful electric telegraph (1837).

**Newton, Isaac (1642-1727),** an English mathematician, devised laws of motion, theorized about gravity, and showed the nature of light and color.

**Pasteur, Louis (1822-95),** a French scientist, proved that disease is spread by bacteria, or germs.

**Rutherford, Sir Ernest (1871-1937),** a New Zealand-born British physicist, was a pioneer in the study of the atom's structure. His work led to the development of nuclear energy.

**Watt, James (1736-1819),** British engineer who improved the steam engine to make it a suitable power plant for all kinds of machinery.

**Wright, Orville (1871-1948) and Wilbur (1867-1912),** two U.S. aeronautical engineers, built and flew (1903) the first successful heavier-than-air aircraft.

## PHILOSOPHERS AND REFORMERS

**Aristotle (384-322 B.C.),** a Greek philosopher, studied under Plato. He opened a school of philosophy in Athens. His work gave rise to the science of logical reasoning.

**Calvin, John (1509-64)**
was a French religious reformer and leader of the Protestant Reformation. He believed that all people, not just bishops and kings, should share in religious and political policy making.

**Confucius (c. 551-c. 480 B.C.)**
was a Chinese philosopher whose teachings on moral responsibility have been a strong influence on Chinese thinking for over 2,000 years.

**Gandhi, Mohandas Karamchand (1869-1948),**
Indian spiritual and political leader, helped free India from British control through nonviolent resistance. He was known as Mahatma, or "Great Soul."

**Gautama, Siddhartha (Buddha) (c. 563-483 B.C.),**
Indian religious teacher, founder of Buddhism, one of the world's great religions. He gave up his life as a prince to become a wandering monk in search of enlightenment.

**Jesus Christ (c. 4 B.C.-c. A.D. 33)**
was the great religious leader on whose teachings the Christian religion was founded.

**Joan of Arc, Saint (c. 1412-1431),**
French national leader and heroine, believed God had chosen her to free France from English rule and led French armies to many victories.

**King, Martin Luther (1929-68)**
was a black American minister and leader of the U.S. civil rights movement. King won the 1964 Nobel Peace Prize, but was assassinated four years later.

**Luther, Martin (1483-1546)**
was a German religious reformer and leader of the Reformation—the religious movement that led to the birth of Protestantism.

**Marx, Karl (1818-83)**
was a German political philosopher and main founder of the socialist and communist movements. Wrote *The Communist Manifesto*, with Friedrich Engels, and *Das Kapital*.

**Montessori, Maria (1870-1952),**
Italian educator and doctor, she designed an educational system to help children develop their intelligence and independence. This system is used throughout the world.

**Mother Teresa of Calcutta (1910-1997)**
was a Roman Catholic nun born in Yugoslavia. She founded a religious order in Calcutta in 1950 called Missionaries of Charity, which has branches in about 30 other countries.

**Muhammad (A.D. 570-632)**
was an Arabian prophet and founder of the Islamic religion. He felt himself called as God's prophet and preached that there is only one God (Allah).

**Nightingale, Florence (1820-1910),**
English nursing pioneer, reformed the nursing profession.

**Pankhurst, Emmeline (1858-1928)**
was an English political reformer. She led the fight for women's right to vote in England.

**Plato (c. 427-c.347BC),**
a Greek philosopher, founded what is probably the first-ever university, known as the Academy. He wrote *The Republic*, in which he outlined the ideal state or society.

**Sanger, Margaret (1883-1966)**
was the American leader of the birth control movement.

**Socrates (c. 469-399 B.C.),**
a Greek philosopher and teacher, devoted himself to seeking truth and goodness.

**Stanton, Elizabeth Cady (1815-1902)**
was a leader of the U.S. women's rights movement. She also worked for the abolition of slavery.

**Wesley, John (1703-91),**
English clergyman, founder of Methodism. He traveled over 5,000 miles a year, preaching.

**Wilberforce, William (1759-1833)**
was an English politician and reformer. He led the fight to abolish slavery in the British Empire.

**Wollstonecraft, Mary (1759-97)**
was an English author who argued that women should have equal rights to men in her book, *A Vindication of the Rights of Women*.

## EXPLORERS

**Amundsen, Roald (1872-1928),**
a Norwegian, discovered the Northwest Passage and was the first man to reach the South Pole (1911).

**Balboa, Vasco Núñez de (1475-1519),**
a Spaniard, was the first European to sight the east coast of the Pacific Ocean (1513).

**Bird, Richard E. (1888-1957),**
a U.S. polar explorer, was the first to fly over the North Pole (1926) and the South Pole (1929).

**Cabot, John (c.1461-98),**
an Italian-born English explorer, claimed North American territory for England.

**Champlain, Samuel de (1567-1635),**
a French explorer, explored the Atlantic coast of Canada and founded Quebec (1608).

**Columbus, Christopher (1451-1506),**
an Italian explorer, discovered the New World while seeking a route to Asia.

**Cook, James (1728-79),**
an English sea captain, was the first to sight Antarctica and explore the Pacific Ocean.

**Cortés, Hernán (1485-1547),**
a Spanish explorer, conquered the Aztec Empire of Mexico (1521).

**Da Gama, Vasco (c.1469-1524),**
Portuguese navigator and explorer, sailed around Africa to India and back to Europe.

**Ericsson, Leif (fl. 900-1000),**
a Viking sailor, was the first European to land in North America (c.1000).

**Livingstone, David (1813-73),**
a Scottish explorer, traveled through much of Africa's interior.

**Magellan, Ferdinand (c.1480-1521),**
a Portuguese explorer, led the first expedition to sail around the world (1519-22). He was killed by natives in the Philippines before the journey was completed.

**Peary, Robert E. (1856-1920),**
a U.S. explorer, claimed to be the first person to reach the North Pole (1909).

**Pizarro, Francisco (c.1475-1541),**
a Spanish explorer, conquered the Inca Empire of Peru (1533).

**Polo, Marco (c.1254-1324),**
a Venetian (Italian) explorer, traveled through Asia and met Kublai Khan, the Mongol emperor.

Elizabeth Cady Stanton began the U.S. women's suffrage movement in 1848.

Gandhi is often called the "father of modern India" for his work in freeing India from British rule.

Vasco da Gama reached India in 1498 by sailing around the Cape of Good Hope in southern Africa.

Henry Morton Stanley, a reporter, found Livingstone (feared dead in Africa) at Lake Tanganyika in 1871.

# ACKNOWLEDGMENTS


## The publishers wish to thank the following for supplying photographs for this book:

ABBREVIATIONS
(*t* = top; *b* = bottom; *c* = center; *l* = left; *r* = right)

PICTURE LIBRARY ABBREVIATIONS
**AAA:** The Ancient Art & Architecture Collection; **AKG:** AKG UK Ltd; **BAL:** The Bridgeman Art Library; **B&C Alexander:** Bryan & Cherry Alexander; **BC:** Bruce Coleman Collection; **EB/JD:** Eye Ubiquitous/James Davis Travel Agency: **ET:** E.T. Archive; **FLPA:** Frank Lane Picture Agency; **FS:** Frank Spooner Pictures; **GI:** Getty Images; **HL:** The Hutchison Library; **NHPA:** Natural History Photographic Agency; **OSF:** Oxford Scientific Films; **Panos:** Panos Pictures; **PE:** Planet Earth Pictures; **Popper:** Popperfoto; **RGA:** The Ronald Grant Archive; **RHPL:** Robert Harding Picture Library; **SP:** Still Pictures; **SPL:** Science Photo Library

Pages: **viii:** Colorific **1: 1** NHPA, GI *(tr)* **1: 2** RHPL *(tr)*, NHPA *(b)* **1: 3** Still Pictures *(b)* **1: 4** SP *(tl)*, RHPL *(bl)*, Panos *(br)* **1: 4/5** RHPL *(tc)* **1: 5** The British Museum *(b)*, AllSport UK *(tr)* **1: 8** Telegraph Colour Library *(tr)* **1: 9** OSF *(tr)* **1: 10** PE *(tr)* **1: 12** NHPA *(tl)*, PE *(tr)* **1: 16** Popper *(tl)*, BC *(cr)*, NHPA *(bl)* **1: 17** The British Museum *(bl)*, AAA *(br)* **1: 19** RHPL *(b)* **1: 20** NHPA *(cr)*, B&C Alexander *(bc)* **1: 21** RHPL *(cl)*. GI *(cr)*, HL *(br)* **1: 22** AKG *(tr, c)*, BAL *(tl, cl, cr, bl, br)* **1: 23** AKG *(tl, cr)*, ET *(tr)*, ©Duane Hanson/Saatchi Collection *(bl)*, BAL *(br)* **1: 24** SP *(tr)*, NHPA *(bl)*, RHPL *(b)* **1: 25** Panos *(b)* **1: 26** HL *(tl/b)*, FS *(tr)* **1: 27** Panos *(tr, bl)*, BAL *(bc)* **1: 28** Portfolio Pictures *(bl)*, SPL *(tr)*, Space Photo Library *(bc)*, NASA *(br)* **1: 32** SPL *(tl, tr)* **1: 34** PE *(tr)*, OSF *(bc)* **1: 35** PE *(bc)*, NHPA *(br)* **1: 36** Colorific *(tl)*, SP *(bc)* **1: 37** RHPL *(tl)*, Colorific *(tr)*, NHPA *(c)* **1: 40** Virgin *(cl)*, Images Colour Library (tr) **1: 43** GI *(tr)* **1: 44** SPL *(tr)* **1: 47** NHPA *(cr)* **2: 1** SPL *(br)* **2: 2** Corbis *(tl)*, SPL *(tr)* **2: 3** Zefa *(br)* **2: 6** EB/JD *(tr)*, RHPL *(cl)*, GI *(b)* **2: 7** GI *(cl)*, EB/JD *(br)* **2: 9** Graham Harrison *(tr)*, GI *(cl, br)* **2: 10** OSF *(cl)* **2: 11** BC *(ct, cb)* **2: 12** Zefa *(tr)*, RHPL *(cl/b)*, Robert Estall Photo Library *(cr)* **2: 13** BC *(cl)*, RHPL *(br)* **2: 14** Panos *(tr)*, HL *(b)* **2: 15** HL *(cl)*, SuperStock *(br)* **2: 16** AllSport UK *(tr)* **2: 17** Ford Motor Company *(tr)* **2: 18** RGA *(tl, ct, cb)*, Portfolio Pictures *(tr)*, SP *(br)* **2: 22** SPL *(l)* **2: 23** The National Museum of Ireland *(tl)*, AAA *(c)*, BAL *(bl)* **2: 24** RHPL *(tr)*, Panos *(b)* **2: 25** GI *(tr, b)*, Panos *(cl)* **2: 27** BC *(tr)*, SP *(cl)*, Image Bank *(b)* **2: 28** BC *(b)* **2: 29** RHPL *(tc)*, GI *(tr, bl)*, RHPL *(br)* **2: 30** Panos *(tr, bl, br)* **2: 31** GI *(c, bcl)*, Zefa *(bl)*, FS *(bcr)*, Rex Features *(br)* **2: 32** Amnesty International *(tl)*, Popper *(tr)*, Corbis *(b)* **2: 33** Corbis *(tl)*, AFP *(bl)*, Camera Press *(br)* **2: 34** Peter Newark Library *(tl)* **2: 38** RHPL *(tr)*, Camera Press *(cl)* **2: 39** Zefa *(tc)*, FS *(tr)*, GI *(c)*, RHPL *(br)* **2: 40** RHPL *(c)* **2: 41** Corbis *(b)* **2: 42** AKG *(tr)* **2: 43** SPL *(tl, bl)* **2: 44** GI *(tr)* **2: 45** Camera Press *(cl, bl)*, AKG *(br)* **2: 47** Corbis *(tr)* GI *(cr)* **2: 48** SPL *(tl)*, AKG *(tr)* **3: 2** Travel Ink *(tr)* **3: 8** RHPL *(br)* **3: 10** Allsport UK/Vandystadt *(bl)*, Performing Arts Library *(br)* **3: 11** EB/JD *(tl)*, Rex Features *(tr)*, Performing Arts Library *(c, br)* **3: 12** Popper *(b)* **3: 13** GI *(tl)* **3: 14** RHPL *(tl)* **3: 18** FS *(tl)*, SPL *(bl)* **3: 19** Farmers Weekly *(br)* **3: 24** Rex Features *(b)* **3: 25** Panos *(tr)*, GI *(b)* **3: 26** Panos *(b)* **3: 27** Panos *(tl)*, GI *(tr)*, Rex Features *(b)* **3: 28** Panos *(br)* **3: 29** Panos *(tl)*, EB/JD *(cl)*, GI *(cr, b)* **3: 30** GI *(l, b)* **3: 31** Simon Farrell *(tr)* **3: 37** GI *(cr)* **3: 38** RHPL *(tr)* **3: 40** Popper *(tl)*, Colorsport *(tr)*, UPI *(cl)* **3: 42** FLPA *(tr)*, GI *(b)* **3: 43** FLPA *(br)* **3: 44** Zefa *(tl)*, GI *(tr)*, Rex Features *(bl)* **3: 45** GI *(tr)*, RHPL *(cl)*, Rex Features *(b)* **4: 1** WJ. Hatt Ltd, The Institute of Explosive *(tl, tc, bl, bc, br)* **4: 2** Topham *(cl)* **4: 3** Popper *(tl, ct, bl)*, Carnera Press *(cb)*, Corbis *(bl)* **4: 6** NHPA *(tr)* **4: 8** FLPA *(cr)* **4: 13** NHPA *(tr)* **4: 14** RHPL *(bl)*, **4: 14/15** GI *(c)* **4: 15** GI *(c)* **4: 16** Telegraph Colour Library *(tr)* **4: 17** Robin Keeley *(tl)*, Topham *(cl)* **4: 18** GI *(tl)* **4: 20** GI *(tr, cl, b)* **4: 21** FS *(tl)*, Popper *(cl)*, RHPL *(cr)* **4: 24** SPL *(tr)* **4: 25** SPL *(tl)* **4: 26** SP *(bl)*, Telegraph Colour Library *(bcl, br)*, GI *(bcr)* **4: 27** Popper *(tr)* **4: 28** Zefa *(tr)*, FS *(cl)*, RHPL *(b)* **4: 29** Popper *(cl)*, GI *(b)* **4: 32** Sonia Halliday Photographs *(cl)* **4: 33** SPL *(tr, bc)*, The Wallace Collection, London *(cl)* **4: 34** RHPL *(cr)*, Topham *(bl)* **4: 35** NHPA *(tl)* **4: 36** Corbis *(cl)*, GI *(b)* **4: 37** Corbis *(tr, cr)* **4: 38** GI *(tr, b)* **4: 39** Popper *(tl)*, RHPL *(cl)*, Panos *(br)* **4: 41** RHPL *(tr)* **4: 42** NHPA *(tr, cl)*, PE *(tl, bcl, bcr)*, GI *(cr)* **4: 45** RHPL *(tr)* **4: 48** FS *(tr)*, GI *(b)* **5: 1** BC *(tr)* **5: 2** Image Bank *(b)* **5: 3** GI *(br)* **5: 4** Transcolour *(tr)* **5: 5** GI *(tr)*, Panos *(bl)*, Zefa *(br)* **5: 6** OSF *(tr)* **5: 7** EB/JD *(t, c, bc)*, Panos *(tc, b)* **5: 8** GI *(tl)*, FS *(cl)* **5: 9** Image Bank *(tc)* **5: 12** Panos *(tr)*, GI *(b)* **5: 13** Panos *(c)* Image Bank *(bl)* **5: 14** Colorific Photo Library *(tl)*, GI *(tr)*, FS *(b)* **5: 15** OSF *(tl)*, Corbis *(tr)*, Panos *(bl)* **5: 16** GI *(cl, bl)*, Panos *(cr)* **5: 18** GI *(tl)* **5: 20** RHPL *(tr)*, Panos *(cr)* **5: 21** OSF *(cr, br)* **5: 22** OSF, BC *(br)* **5: 24** FS *(tr)* **5: 25** BAL *(tr)* **5: 26** GI *(cl, bl)*, The Houghton's Horses *(br)* **5: 27** GI *(tr)* **5: 28** RHPL *(cl)*, GI *(b)* **5: 29** FLPA *(tr)*, GI *(cl)*, Network Photography/Mike Abraham *(bl)* **5: 30** GI *(b)* **5: 31** FS *(cr)*, John Ferro Sims *(bl)* **5: 32** GI *(tr, b)*, Panos *(cl)* **5: 33** RHPA *(cr)*, Zefa *(b)* **5: 34** Zefa *(tr)* **5: 35** GI *(tr, cl)*, Image Bank *(bl)*, Colorific Photo Library *(cb)* **5: 37** Panos *(cl)*, PE *(bl)*, GI *(br)* **5: 38** SPL *(tl)* **5: 40** EB/JD *(tl)*, BAL *(b)* **5: 41** RHPL *(tl)*, Zefa *(tr, bl)*, The Research House *(cl)* **5: 42** Image Bank *(tl)* **5: 45** Zefa *(tr, cr)*, Corbis *(tl)*, Image Bank *(cl)*, OSF *(bl, bc)* **5: 46** Image Bank *(tl)* **6: 4** SPL *(tr)* **6: 5** HL *(cl)*, Panos *(bl)*, RHPL *(br)* **6: 9** Image Bank *(tr)* **6: 10** Panos *(tr)* **6: 11** Alpha *(c)*, A.C. Edwards *(b)* **6: 12** Glaxo Group Research *(tr)* **6: 13** SPL *(tr, b)* **6: 15** AAA *(cr, br)* **6: 16** Telegraph Colour Library *(tl)* **6: 17** South American Pictures *(tr)*, Spectrum Colour Library *(cl)*, Panos *(bl)* **6: 18** SPL *(l)* **6: 19** SPL *(l)*, Leo Electron Microscope *(tr)*, Leica UK *(bc)* **6: 21** RHPL *(tr)*, Panos *(b)* **6: 22** HL *(c)* **6: 23** Spectrum Colour Library *(tl)*, FS *(tr)*, HL *(bc)* **6: 24** PE *(bl)* **6: 25** OSF *(tr)* **6: 26** SP *(tl)* **6: 31** OSF *(br)* **6: 36** Zefa *(t)*, Redferns *(cl, bl, br)* **6: 37** RHPL *(b)* **6: 38** Edinburgh University *(cr)*, Keith Saunders Photography *(bc)* **6: 43** Corbis *(tr)* **6: 45** FS *(bl)* **6: 47** Spectrum Colour Library *(tc, c)*, FS *(bl)* **6: 48** Panos *(cl, b)* **7: 1** Panos *(tr)*, HL *(bl)* **7: 2** NHPA *(bl)* **7: 3** Panos *(tl)*, HL *(tr)*, Zefa *(bl)* **7: 4** Popper *(tr)* **7: 5** SP *(tr)* **7: 8** SPL *(tr)* **7: 9** AllSport *(cr)* Topham *(b)* **7: 10** Topham *(tl)* **7: 11** AllSport UK *(tr, cr)* **7: 13** SPL *(tl)* **7: 15** HL *(tr)*, Panos *(cl, c)* **7: 16** Polaroid *(cl)*, Ixus *(bl)*, BAL *(b)* **7: 17** Science & Society Picture Library *(tr)*, Nikon UK *(br)* **7: 18** HL *(tr)* **7: 21** The Kobal Collection *(bl)* **7: 24** ICI *(b)* **7: 25** NHPA *(tl, tr)* **7: 26** Corbis *(t)* **7: 27** HL *(b)* **7: 29** AAA *(cl)* **7: 31** Popper *(cr)* **7: 35** NHPA *(cl)* **7: 36** PE *(tr)* **7: 38** SP *(tl)*, Jean-Loup Charmet *(tr)*, Popper *(bl)* **7: 39** HL *(b)* **7: 40** BAL *(cr, bl)* **7: 42** GI *(cr)* **7: 48** Rex Features *(tl)*, Popper *(tr)*, GI *(cl)* **8: 1** PE *(tr)* **8: 2** NHPA *(bl)*, HL *(br)* **8: 4** GI *(tl)*, HL *(bc)* **8: 5** SPL *(tl, cl)*, The Kobal Collection *(tc)*. Honda Motor Company *(tr)* **8: 6**: NHPA *(tr)* **8: 7** NASA *(tr)* **8: 9** Zefa *(tr)*, GI *(cr)* **8: 10** Novosti London *(tr)*, RHPL *(b)* **8: 11** HL *(br)* **8: 12** Rex Features *(tl)*, Novosti London *(cl)*, HL *(bl, br)* **8: 14** GI *(tr, b)* **8: 15** RHPL *(bl)*, FLPA *(br)* **8: 16** AKG *(tl)*, Rex Features *(tr)*, *(c)* Andy Goldworthy *(cl)*, GI *(b)* **8: 17** GI *(tl, cl)*, HL *(br)* **8: 18** HL *(cr)*, Spectrum Colour Library *(br)* **8: 22** Zefa *(tr)* **8: 25** RHPL *(tr)*, AAA *(c)*, Christie's Images *(cr)* **8: 26** GI *(tr, b)* **8: 29** Travel Ink *(tl)* **8: 30** BAL *(tr)*, Mary Evans Picture Library *(br)* **8: 31** SPL *(tl)*, AKG *(b)* **8: 32** OSF *(tc)* **8: 33** NHPA *(tr)* **8: 34** Zefa *(b)* **8: 35** Topham *(tr)* **8: 39** Popper *(b)* **8: 40** RHPL *(cl, tr)*, GI *(b)* **8: 41** FS *(bl)*, RHPL *(cr)* **8: 42** South American Library *(tr, cl, b)* **8: 43** HL *(tl)*, South American Library *(bl)*, Panos *(br)* **8: 44** Panos *(tl, b)*, South American Library *(tr)* **8: 45**. South American Library *(tr, c)*, HL *(b)* **8: 46** Panos *(bl)* **8: 47** Panos *(tl, c)*, HL *(tr)* **9: 1** SPL *(tr)* **9: 2** SPL *(l)* **9: 4** GI *(tr)*, HL *(cl)*. RHPL *(b)* **9: 5** HL *(b)* **9: 7** NHPA *(tl)* **9: 9** Sporting Pictures *(tr)*, AllSport UK *(br)* **9: 10** Sporting Pictures *(tc)* **9: 13** NHPA *(tr)* **9: 14** SPL *(tl)*, GI *(tr)* **9: 16** HL *(cl)*, Panos *(bl)* **9: 18** AKG *(tr)*, RHPL *(b)* **9: 20** RHPL **9: 22** SPL *(b)* **9: 23** Zefa *(tr)* **9: 24** Mary Evans Picture Library *(tl)*, British Telecom *(cl)*, GI *(bl)* **9: 25** Corbis *(tr, br)*, Philips UK *(cl)* **9: 27** Simmons Ltd *(tc)*, SPL *(br)* **9: 29** AKG *(tr)*, SPL *(bl)*, RHPL *(br)* **9: 34** Topham *(tr)* **9: 35** Panos *(cl)*. RGA *(cr)*, RHPL *(b)* **9: 36** GI *(tr)* **9: 37** Panos *(b)* **9: 40** SPL *(cl)* **9: 41** FS *(br)* **9: 43** Telegraph Colour Library *(tr)* **9: 44** Greyhound Ltd *(tr)* **9: 45** GI *(bl)* **9: 46** Popper *(cl)*, RHPL *(tr)*, British Tourist Authority *(b)* **9: 47** British Tourist Authority *(tl)*, HL *(bl)*, RHPL *(br)* **9: 48** FS *(cr)*, Popper *(b)* **10: 1** Panos *(tr)*, RHPL *(bl, br)* **10: 2** RHPL **(tl, cl)**. Zefa *(br)* **10: 3** RHPL *(cl, br)* **10: 4** RHPL *(tl, cl)*, Corbis *(cr)*, Redfern *(b)* **10: 5** SPL *(tl)* **10: 6** Popper *(b)* **10: 7** Sanyo UK *(tl)*, SPL *(tr, cl)*, Sony *(br)* **10: 10** HL *(tl)* **10: 14** Topham *(br)* **10: 15** HL *(tc)* **10: 16** Corbis *(tl)* **10: 17** SPL *(tr)* **10: 19** SPL *(tc)* **10: 21** SPL *(tl)* **10: 25** RHPL *(tr)*, SPL *(b)* **10: 27** NHPA *(tc)* **10: 28** Corbis *(tr)*, Corbis *(b)* **10: 29** GI *(tl)*, Corbis *(tr)*, Popper *(bl)*, Corbis *(cr)* **10: 33** Corbis *(bl)* **10: 34** PE *(br)* **10: 35** SPL *(tr, bl)* **10: 36**: Marwell Zoo *(br)*

## Illustrators

Julian Baker Illustration, Julian Baum, Michelle Brand, Andy Burton, Tom Connell, Maggie Downer, Richard Draper, Andrew Farmer, Chris Forsey, Mick Gillah, Trevor Hill, Karen Hiscock, Christian Hook, Kevin Jones Associates, Ruth Lindsay, Ceri Llewellyn, Kevin Maddison, Nicki Palin, Peter Ross, Peter Sarson, Mike Saunders, Ron Tiner, Martin Woodward, *Black Hat*: Kevin Lyles, *Blue Chip*: Keith Harmer, *David Lewis Agency*: Mark Stacey, *J.M. & A*: Steinar Lund, *Linda Rogers Associates*: Peter Dennis, *Linden Artists*: Lindsay Graham, Richard Hook, Sebastian Quigley, Clive Spong, *Specs Art*: Richard Berridge, *Virgil Pomfret*: Luigi Galanti, *W.L.A*: Cy Baker, Derick Bown, Robin Budden, Robin Carter, Barry Croucher, Sandra Doyle, Brin Edwards, David Hardy, Dan Harvey, Philip Hood, Ian Jackson, Bridgette Jones, Rachel Lockwood, Pond/Giles, Jonathan Potter, Steve Roberts, Andrew Robinson, Mike Rowe, Chris Shields, Paul Staveley, Mark Stewart, Mike Taylor, Richard Tibbitts, Chris Turnbull, Simon Turvey, David Woods

## The publishers would also like to thank the following for their help in supplying information used as visual reference:

Pages: **1: 6–7** Boeing Aircraft Corporation (Boeing 747); **1: 11** Zoological Society of London (fire salamander cutaway); **1: 17** Geoscan Research (scanner); **1: 19** Ove Arup & Partners (Sydney Opera House); **1: 30–31** W.M. Keck Observatory (Keck observatory); **2: 14–15** John Willoughby, The Mustang Owners Club of Great Britain, Selby (Mustang); **4: 2** Fullwood Ltd (milking shed); **4: 46** Bell Helicopter Textron (helicopter cutaway); **5: 4** Dyson Appliances Ltd (Dyson vacuum cleaner cutaway); **5: 6** The Hovercraft Museum Trust; **6: 2–3** Otis plc, Ove Arup & Partners (elevator); **6: 12–13** Picker International Ltd, Siemens Medical Engineering (CAT scanner); **7: 4** Nuclear Electric (nuclear reactor); **7: 8** British Petroleum (platform); **7: 9–11** Olympic Museum; **8: 25** Balco Ltd (electroplating system); **9: 26** British Telecom (wall telephone); **9: 41** Ford Motor Company (people carrier)